Shake Off the Lies

Untangling the Worst for God's Best

Heather V. Shore

Shake Off the Lies: Untangling the Worst for God's Best

By Heather V. Shore

Sun Creek Press

Broken Arrow, OK 740111

© 2025 Heather V. Shore

Cover design by Oluwatosin Adebayo.

ISBN 979-8-218-56625-8

Table of Contents

Foreword

I have had the great delight and joy of knowing Heather Shore for a solid decade. I've known Heather as one of her pastors at our Rockland Community Church in Golden, Colorado, as a coworker in our wedding and memorial ministry at said church, as a fellow believer in Christ Jesus, and as a very good friend. During our friendship, Heather and I enjoyed many a conversation about life, love and marriage, relationships, heartaches and pain, hopes and dreams, children, work, ministry, etc. However, most of our conversations have centered upon Jesus, the movement of the Holy Spirit, and Heather's ministry calling.

You guessed it right. I know Heather well. In fact, in many ways, I consider myself to be a "spiritual father" in her life!

Allow me to share the following about Heather . . .

First, Heather has a deep-rooted, time-tested love for the second Person of the Trinity! In addition, anyone who knows Heather would say with me that she enjoys a Spirit-led faith in Jesus!

What Heather talks about is what she lives into and lives out of! In fact, in all Heather does, the Holy Spirit oozes out of her. She is as Spirit driven as anyone I know.

Second, Heather truly desires that all people in her world would know Jesus as Savior and follow Him as Lord. This heavenly hope of Heather is as important to her as are her two children. And just as a side note, Harrison and Maddie mean the world to Momma Heather!

Third, and finally, so important to Heather's heart is this: She deeply cares about the Lord's people, especially those who have suffered some type of harsh trauma in their lives. That is, Heather desires to see people free from the bondage that keeps them from living the Spirit-filled life the Lord intended.

With that third thought in mind, I have had the privilege of walking with Heather through many of life's challenges hand-grenaded toward her by the enemy. I have walked with Heather through gut-wrenching heartaches, through a heartbreaking divorce, through sad friendship betrayals, through a host of painful losses in her life as well as many other challenging situations.

With all that Heather has experienced, I can say that Heather never wavered from her faith in Jesus. She may have asked Him why or what lessons there were to be learned. She may have cried her million tears. She may have shouted in frustration. But Heather never wavered from walking with Jesus. Hurt and sad, but still strong in Jesus. In fact, I would be so bold to say that Heather is way stronger in her faith today than when I first met her (and her faith was quite rock solid then).

With the above in mind, and in my estimation, I believe that Heather's strong faith amid these "hand grenades" tossed by the enemy, along with the leading of the Holy Spirit, gives her the unique authority to speak on the topic contained within this book! In addition, this book will challenge the reader to examine his or her own life and all that he or she has experienced. It will not be an easy challenge, but it will be more than worthwhile!

If you would like to experience the fullness of the Spirit in living the life the Lord desires for you, then this book is for you. If you want the Spirit to ooze out of you in all you do despite your challenging times, then this book is for you. And if you wish to be free from the bondage of those past traumas that keeps you from living in Christ Jesus, then this book is definitely for you. Be greatly fed to enjoy what the Lord desires you to experience! And be blessed by Him who truly is the author of the words contained within!

Retired Pastor Edward C. Lange

October 22, 2025

Arvada, Colorado

Introduction

This book is for those who have survived life's abuses. Writing your ending is not your job—it's God's job. His story always ends with life, healing and tears being wiped from every eye.

Every one of us will encounter a lie at some point in our lives. To believe a lie is to believe a false narrative or false truth about a situation, someone, or something. The goal of lying is always to mislead a person. When we run into lies, we have a choice. Do we believe the narrative being presented to us, or do we believe something else? Each day, several lies about who we are as people, what is going on in our world, and in many places are presented to us as "truth." In each instance, at the core, you have to decide: What do you believe? How do you discern the truth from a lie? What lies might you be believing not only about yourself but about the world around you?

God is a God of truth. He is the author of truth, of justice, and not of confusion. He speaks from his mercy seat to each of us, calling us further into his kingdom. If we are open to hearing about the truth, we will start to realize the amount of lies in the atmosphere. Lies told to us every day to confuse us, to belittle us, to put us down, and to make us smaller than what we are called to be. So many of the lies told to us are meant to derail us from our purpose. Our purpose as Christians is to bring glory to God and to be his hands and feet on earth until he returns. If that is your purpose, how are the lies you're believing holding you back from walking this out? This book is about some of the lies that hold us back from living the truth of who God is and how to boldly walk out our purpose.

Let's face the lies we are believing. Let's take our thoughts captive, learn to walk in power and authority, and take back the territory from the enemy. Only then can we be the lions and lionesses God has called us to be.

Lie #1: God Isn't Good

"Shake off the lies that you have let settle into your
heart like a poison."
—*Nate Johnston*

One Sunday at church, the pastor said, "You can't sin

unless you believe a lie." It hit me like a ton of bricks. I realized I

had believed so many lies because of different influences in my

life, like lust and rebellion. But most of all, I didn't believe God

was good. How could he be after walking through divorce and

losing so much in my life? Having to rebuild your life after grief is

hard. Grief comes in so many ways, through the loss of loved ones,

the loss of marriage, the loss of a job, or a change in our

circumstances. We must even grieve our expectations. You may

expect to stay married, but what if the person you are married to

walks away and chooses a different life? This among so many

other life circumstances can cause you to believe that God isn't good. Why would he allow suffering and broken-heartedness? That's what we are here to unpack.

As God healed my heart from the many—and I mean many—lies I believed, I truly came to understand his goodness and how he earnestly desires to shower us with his goodness. It came as a surprise, to be completely honest. Growing up under a religious spirit had caused me to believe faith was all about performance. Even though James 1:17 says, "Every good and perfect gift is from above, coming down from the Father of the heavenly lights, who does not change like shifting shadows," I had a very hard time believing, let alone understanding, this verse. Multiple life circumstances had come my way, some through my own choices and some not my own, and it hurt. It hurt so badly. Walking out of a marriage that was toxic and emotionally negligent led me to project my expectations in human relationships and my shortcomings onto God. God isn't like us at all! And thank goodness he isn't. He is kind, merciful, loving, filled with justice, and he wants to take care of us. In my mind, though, nobody wanted to take care of me, so why would God want to do such a thing? As you can see, there were so many lies I had to unpack to walk in freedom in this area. (Thank goodness he is a God who cannot lie, as Numbers 23:19 reminds us).

Miraculously, the Lord slowly walked me into freedom, nudging me to read and consume his Word, spend hours in prayer, be alone with him, and worship him. These activities might sound religious, but when the presence of God shows up, you want to spend time with him. Hard to explain until you've experienced it. When I started trusting God could be good, things started to get exciting. That's when he started asking me to partner with him in various aspects of my life. Whether it was praying for someone at Walmart, showing up for my kids and unpacking their emotions, buying a present and loving on people, my faith became fun. Each day has become an adventure. When not in the storm, I wake up wondering, *What we are going to do today and how can I be present with him?* Walking with Jesus really should be fun and exciting. Because when we really sit down and partner with him in our faith and undoing all the lies, it becomes a fun adventure of seeking his kingdom above all else (Matthew 6:33).

What Makes the Lies We Believe So Powerful

According to Michael Desgrosseilliers, president of Elijah House Ministries,

> God honors the decisions we make even when those decisions aren't good. We were created to be sons and daughters for all eternity, not robotic entities that have no will. So, when we decide in our heart to agree with a lie, God allows us to do so because that is our choice.

> Jesus said in Matthew 18:18 (NKJV), "Assuredly, I say to you, whatever you bind on earth will be bound in heaven, and whatever you loose on earth will be loosed in heaven." Lies are heart decisions we made as a result of hurt. When we "loose" a lie in our life, it is also "loosed" in the spiritual realm. It is no small thing to agree with a lie, and we get what we agree with.[1]

---

[1] Michael Desgrosseilliers, newsletter email to author, June 11, 2024.

Here are some common lies people believe:

- "I will not be close to anyone, because if I do, I'm just going to be hurt."
- "I can't trust anyone to take care of me. I have to take care of myself."
- "My pain will never be healed. I will always hurt. Not even God can help me."
- "My past will keep me from going far in life."
- "I'm not good enough; therefore, I'm not lovable."

Lies can have a tremendous impact in our lives because God made us powerful. When we say yes to something, that thing—good or bad—is allowed to influence us.

But just as we come into agreement with a lie, we can choose to come out of agreement with it. When we do, God releases us from the lie's power and influence over us.

He certainly can step in and destroy the lies we believe. But He wants us to choose to come out of agreement with them and agree with His words instead. He wants us to choose life, as Deuteronomy 30:19 talks about (NKJV): "I call heaven and earth as witnesses today against you, that I have set before you life and death, blessing and cursing; therefore choose life, that both you and your descendants may live."

One example I personally needed to come out of agreement with was anger. As I realized the level of anger I held in my body from unhealthy relationships and it became clear there needed to be a new path forward because the current one wasn't working. I was projecting the anger onto God not believing in his goodness. Rashes were breaking out all over my body from stored-up emotions. My friend Jodi, in one of our conversations, even had some words of wisdom about loving people well, maintaining healthy boundaries, and walking out our anger. Here are the notes I took during our conversation:

It's His loving-kindness that brings us to repentance. I pray that you will be able to step into a place where you can see but are able to live with

His love, that it starts to convict people in our lives who don't value the Holy Spirit in good ways. Ultimately, the *only* responsibility you have is to love. Sometimes, it's easier said than done—keeping opinions to yourself and praying blessings over them when you don't want to. An example of a quick simple prayer is, "Lord, bless them with the revelation knowledge of who you are. Open their eyes so they can see you clearly. Bless them with your love, joy, and peace." Another prayer would be "Encounter them, visit them in the night hour, when they are in the shower or even driving in the car." Simple prayers. Don't overthink it and be careful not to pray soulful prayers; it's easy to do when we are in our emotions. I pray the Lord will give you creative ways to interact with people. That he would show you what words would penetrate or cause action. I also pray that He will show you what boundaries in every relationship should look like. Jodi gave all of this wisdom in a meaningful conversation we had around forgiveness and the goodness of God.

The Truth: God Is Good

God's goodness conveys his generosity. When we believe the lie that God isn't good, we miss his goodness and the ability to see his generosity in our lives. God has so many characteristics that get misconstrued because of our own vantage points. When we don't see rightly (or are asking in our humanness for the ability to see as God sees, especially others), we don't see his love, grace, mercy, and long-suffering for others and ourselves. When we look throughout the Bible, there are multiple stories of God's goodness:

- Creation (Genesis)

- God's provision of a ram in the story of Abraham and Isaac (Genesis)

- Joseph in Potiphar's house—With one dream God was able to pull Joseph out of prison and set him in a place of honor. (Genesis)

- Ruth and Boaz—Through Ruth's obedience, the line of Jesus was continued. (Ruth)

- God's forgiveness of David after his adultery (Psalm 51)

- Elijah and the widow of Zarephath (1 Kings)

- Hezekiah's healing (2 Kings)

- The parable of the prodigal son (Luke 15:11–32)

- God proclaiming to Moses that he will show his goodness to him (Exodus 33:18–19)

- The fruit of the Holy Spirit, including goodness, God's love, grace, mercy, and long-suffering (Galatians 5:22–23)

None of these biblical examples convey stories of heroes and heroines simply believing in the goodness of God and hoping to see his goodness in the land of the living. They knew the goodness of God in tangible ways that made their faith come alive supernaturally. We see the manifestations of God's goodness in various forms—from the creation of the world to the redemption of sinners—and in each of these biblical examples we see God's hand of redemption and forgiveness. When we really study the goodness of God and his mercy, love, and faithfulness, we get a glimpse of his true nature, and that starts to unravel the lie that God isn't good.

Scripture Verses About the Goodness of God

"Every good gift and every perfect present comes from heaven; it comes down from God, the Creator of the heavenly lights, who does not change or cause darkness by turning" (James 1:17 GNT).

"Oh, give thanks to the LORD, for He is good! For His mercy endures forever" (1 Chronicles 16:34 NKJV).

"The LORD, the LORD God, merciful and gracious, longsuffering, and abounding in goodness and truth" (Exodus 34:6 NKJV).

"Do you have no regard for the wealth of His kindness and tolerance and patience [in withholding His wrath]? Are you [actually] unaware *or* ignorant [of the fact] that God's kindness leads you to repentance [that is, to change your inner self, your old way of thinking—seek His purpose for your life]?" (Romans 2:4 AMP).

Spiritual Warfare—Fighting Back

You can't sin unless you believe a lie—whether it's a lie about God, yourself, your circumstances, life, etc. Sin entered the world because Eve believed a lie. If she hadn't listened to the enemy, sin wouldn't have entered the world. Lies are very powerful and destructive and lead to death. When we uncover the lies and agreements we're believing, it leads to freedom. We learn how to combat the lies with the truth, and it expands our capacity for greater freedom and confidence. How does one combat the lies? Through Scripture, self-reflection, memorizing the Word, prayer, Christian mentors, etc. Ask yourself these questions to battle the lie that God isn't good:

1. What lies are you believing? Sit down, get quiet, and ask the Lord to reveal any anything you are believing that goes against God's goodness in your life.

2. Goodness of God comes through renewing your mind on his word and through thankfulness. What is one

good thing in your life you can thank God for each day? Renew your mind by thinking on these things daily.

3. Ask the Holy Spirit to meet you during your quiet time. Ask the Holy Spirit to reveal one lie you are believing that goes against the goodness of God. What is it? What does God's word say to tangibly combat the lies that he isn't good?

4. It's like developing muscles. The more you meditate on the Word of God, the more it sinks into your heart. How can you develop more spiritual muscles?

Prayer

Show us, Lord, where we believe and have come into agreement with lies that speak against the goodness of God. Help us to untwist anything deceiving us, and help us come into right alignment with you. Show us the truth of who we are and whose we are. Help us to dig up the roots and replace lies with the truth. We are each uniquely created in your image. May we believe this to be true and see your truth in each area of our lives.

Lie #2: God Doesn't Heal

"Repent of the lies and replace it with the truth."
—Dave Hayes, the Praying Medic

The Lord led me through a season of coming into an understanding what it means to be healed in the Bible. What does healing mean, how does it work, and can we encounter it today? Through multiple teachings of other people with healing ministries, I started to encounter different viewpoints and translations of what it means to be whole, healed, and delivered.

God's Will Is for Us to Be Healed

One of the viewpoints I came to understand was that God's will is for us to be healed. This was new to me and one I've struggled to grasp at times. For so long, I had believed the lie that God only heals certain people. We don't always know why healing takes place, and there will always be the mystery of God and some things will remain unexplained, especially in this area. Praying Medic says,

Jesus healed everyone who came to him for healing and never turned anyone away. It is God's will for us to be healed. It's part of the Great Commission. The Great Commission is to preach the Kingdom to every creature.

Jesus told the disciples, "I want you to give them something to eat. The little boy had 5 loaves and 2 fish. Jesus blesses this gift and breaks the bread, and the food is given out to the large crowd. There are parallel passages in Mark 6, John 6, Matthew 14 where Jesus prayed over it and gave the 2 fishes and loaves back to the disciples. By faith he had them will pass it out to see what would happen. As they passed it out, the food multiplied. This event in the Bible tested the disciples to see if they would walk in His ways. Do we understand God's nature and His Kingdom? Faith is the issue in all of this. Everything we do in the authority and power of God, we do by faith. Faith is what works and brings miracles. If you are afraid, doubt and don't believe it, it will be hard to see miracles. We need to trust God to multiply it, and he did in the loaves and fishes' story.

One of the keys to this parable around food multiplication is your heart. Is your heart to help people in need? God multiples what you have. If your heart is to only take care of yourself, he may bless part of that, but if your heart is to help others and be a light on the hill in the coming days, God's blessing will be more than what we can imagine. We need to trust God to meet our needs because He will blow your mind on what he will do.

Power and Authority

Another viewpoint regarding God's healing involves His power and authority. What do you believe about the authority God has given you, as stated in Matthew 1:14–20. If you believe and have faith that the power of God will leave you, flowing out of your body to create a miracle, it will happen. When you have faith, it leads to supernatural events. Faith is the confidence that the miracles you read about in the Bible can happen in your life too. God's promises are yes and amen, and for those who believe, anything can happen (Mark 9:23).

Power is letting God's power flow out of your body. Authority is knowing who you are as a disciple of Jesus or child of God. It's an issue of knowing who you are, which means knowing your identity. We are ambassadors of God. We are to make known to the world his kingdom, his goodness, his compassion, and to be healed and live an abundant life. Authority can be used to cast out demons and remove things such as lies, beliefs, and vows that are not supposed to be there. In my journey I learned how to command things to leave the body, such as evil spirits, tumors, and diseases. We can command them to go. Jesus said he can do nothing himself but only what the Father is doing. Ask God,

- How do I do this?
- What is the key to what is going on inside this person?
- What is the name of the demon controlling the person?
- What are you missing? In other words, what thing are you not picking up on that could be causing this issue?

- What's the key to seeing whatever is bothering them to leave? Ask the Holy Spirit to show you what's going on with this individual.

During this time, I attended Randy Clark's Healing Conference. His healing resources are phenomenal, and he had a valid point: What am I expecting in life? What lie am I believing that is preventing the Holy Spirit to work a miracle in our lives? He said, "I want you expecting to receive! God reveals himself as 'the Lord who heals you.' The basis of healing is the covenant, and signs and wonders are part of each covenant."

In Isaiah 53:3–5 we see that God has taken our infirmities (sicknesses, diseases, *choli* in Hebrew) and carried our sorrows (pain, or *makov* in Hebrew). But he was pierced for our transgressions, he was crushed for our iniquities; the punishment was upon him that would bring us peace, and by his wounds we are healed.

What struck me about each area of healing that I learned was what the Lord carried for us at the cross. It wasn't just our sin. He carried our sorrows—our broken hearts, dashed hopes and dreams, expectations that didn't turn out, our failures, the idols we chased—and he sacrificed so we could be coheirs with him because he hates death. I had always thought of him sacrificing just for our sin and even sickness, not our sorrows. He cared about those too!

I had lost all expectations when it came to healing and had a hard time receiving anything. Instead of letting God in, I treated him like a genie, asking and begging him to heal me. I wasn't expecting goodness, righteousness, and other fruit of the Spirit to develop in me as a result of the disease I experienced. He took all the sorrow—hopelessness, depression, heaviness, all of it—and healed me! He carries all our infirmities and makes us new. By not carrying around all of the heaviness and sickness in my body, it brought fun back into my life. Now he makes life fun and adventurous!

Healing in the Kingdom

Healing occurs through the sacrifice of Christ's body on the cross and is a part of the atonement. Jesus is your physician, and through our inheritance in him, he is already healing you. Psalm 103:1–5 (AMP) says, "Bless and affectionately praise the LORD, O my soul, and all that is [deep] within me, bless His holy name. Bless and affectionately praise the LORD, O my soul, and do not forget any of His benefits; *Who forgives all your sins, Who heals all your diseases*; Who redeems your life from the pit, Who crowns you [lavishly] with lovingkindness and tender mercy; Who satisfies your years with good things, So that your youth is renewed like the [soaring] eagle" (emphasis mine).

He renews and transforms us, and it is God's will for us to be well. Don't always automatically come into agreement with what the doctor says without also putting your experience up against the Word of God, for the Word of God is true. God wants you well! Miracles still happen. Say you were blind, and he gives you a creative miracle and re-establishes your sight. This is because we are healed by his stripes and his power is inside us. When Isaiah 53 says we are healed, it means we are healed in the spirit realm now! We are supposed to live in the spiritual realm because the power of Jesus dwells in us. We are the people of God who are to walk out believing God has healed and will heal us.

You can absolutely heed doctors' advice. And if the doctor diagnoses you with something serious, do all the things to get well. The problem is that people claim the disease as their identity and then don't walk out the life God has for them. A perfect example is that everyone has anxiety. You don't anxiety - you have a worry problem and don't know how to take your thoughts captive to the authority of Christ. Anxiety, worry, etc. are the opposite of peace. Does this mean you don't seek out therapy, healing and deliverance? Nope, you absolutely do, but what you say over yourself matters. You either agree with what God says or you agree with what a doctor says. Christians are some of the sickest people because they don't live out what they preach.

Isaiah 53:3–5 (AMP) tell us,

He was despised and rejected by men, a
Man of sorrows and pain and acquainted with grief;
and like One from whom men hide their faces He
was despised, and we did not appreciate His worth
or esteem Him. But [in fact] He has borne our
griefs, and He has carried our sorrows and pains;
Yet we [ignorantly] assumed that He was stricken,
struck down by God and degraded and humiliated
[by Him]. But He was wounded for our
transgressions, He was crushed for our wickedness
[our sin, our injustice, our wrongdoing]; The
punishment [required] for our well-being fell on
Him, and by His stripes (wounds) we are healed.

In Greek, salvation means wholeness. Healing doesn't happen from the outside in; it happens from the inside out and comes from your faith. Faith is the bridge between the unseen and the seen—where what God has promised becomes reality. The law of faith is found in Hebrews 11:1 (ESV): "faith is the assurance of things hoped for, the conviction of things not seen." This includes what is not revealed to the senses. Are you going to let the enemy take your faith from you? Hebrews 11:6 (AMP) says, "But without faith it is impossible to [walk with God and] please Him, for whoever comes [near] to God must [necessarily] believe that God exists and that He rewards those who [earnestly and diligently] seek Him."

God forgives all your sins, and then he doesn't remember them. Sometimes you have to ask the Lord to help you forget the iniquities. In Mark 11:22–24 (AMP), "Jesus replied, 'Have faith in God [constantly]. I assure you and most solemnly say to you, whoever says to this mountain, "Be lifted up and thrown into the sea!" and does not doubt in his heart [in God's unlimited power], but believes that what he says is going to take place, it will be done for him [in accordance with God's will]. For this reason, I am telling you, whatever things you ask for in prayer [in accordance with God's will], believe [with confident trust] that you have received them, and they will be *given* to you."

Part of building up your faith muscle to truly believe that healing is possible is being transformed by the renewing of your mind through the Word of God. When it comes to healing in life, you've got to unplug from worldly sources and plug into the healing power of God. Take your authority in the spiritual realm and say, "Enough! In the name of Jesus, I command you [whatever the sickness or evil spirit may be] to leave. You have no legal authority or right, and I'm commanding you to go in the name of Jesus. Not leaving here until it's done! Nothing by any means will harm me." Then you continue to pray until it's gone.

One example is a woman who prayed over her son for twenty minutes until the sickness left his body. The more you speak healing over your life, the more you'll believe it! Matthew 11:12 (AMP) tells us. "The kingdom of heaven suffers violent assault, and violent men seize it by force [as a precious prize]."

Submit yourself to God and resist the devil, and he will flee. James 4:7 says, "Submit yourselves, then, to God. Resist the devil, and he will flee from you." Unbelief and unforgiveness are the big offenses keeping healing away. Let them go! Bless those who persecute you. Your emotions won't catch up until your thoughts do, so tell God, "Lord, I bless that person." After walking through forgiveness and asking the Lord to heal the wounds in your soul, do you see yourself healed? There is power in the imagination and in speaking life before you see the fruit. As Proverbs 18:21 reminds us, "The tongue has the power of life and death, and those who love it will eat its fruit." Speak healing over yourself, your family and your situations. See yourself healed! What does it look like? Each of the areas the Lord has healed for humanity has brought about a new understanding, allowing healing to unlock its true potential in our lives.

The Truth: God Does Heal

When we come out of agreement with the lies we believe, we allow the Spirit to flow through and heal us. God wants to heal us and help us find freedom in every area of life. The Bible says he sanctifies us from glory to glory: "But we all, with unveiled face, beholding as in a mirror the glory of the Lord, are being transformed into the same image from glory to glory, just as from the Lord, the Spirit" (2 Corinthians 3:18 NKJV). If his goal is to transform us, why wouldn't he heal us? Healing is part of the cross. It comes in many different forms and ways. When we look at the healing ministry of Jesus, he healed in many ingenious ways. He used mud on a blind man's eyes to bring him sight. People touched his cloak, and they were healed instantly. The power of God left him and instantly healed a woman with the issue of blood. He took away sadness and through his stories healed people's wounds. Some men with leprosy came by and begged God to heal him. He told them to go show themselves to the priests that they were healed. Only one came back to thank him, as it says in Luke 17:14–19: "When he saw them, he said, 'Go, show yourselves to the priests.' And as they went, they were cleansed. One of them, when he saw he was healed, came back, praising God in a loud voice. He threw himself at Jesus' feet and thanked him—and he was a Samaritan. Jesus asked, 'Were not all ten cleansed? Where are the other nine? Has no one returned to give praise to God except this foreigner?' Then he said to him, 'Rise and go; your faith has made you well.'" When God heals, we are to be thankful and not take it for granted. He is so gracious to us and wants to shower his goodness and love on us, and one of the many beautiful ways he does this is through healing.

What is possibly holding you back from this truth permeating your being? There are countless stories in the Bible and stories from today that showcase the amazing healing power of the cross. There truly is nothing like the blood of Jesus to wipe away all sins, inequities, disease, sorrows, and wounds. He is so good, and he wants you to walk in wholeness and healing today.

Scripture Verses About God's Healing

"Jesus replied, 'Have faith in God [constantly]. I assure you and most solemnly say to you, whoever says to this mountain, "Be lifted up and thrown into the sea!" and does not doubt in his heart [in God's unlimited power], but believes that what he says is going to take place, it will be done for him [in accordance with God's will]. For this reason I am telling you, whatever things you ask for in prayer [in accordance with God's will], believe [with confident trust] that you have received them, and they will be *given* to you'" (Mark 11:22–24 AMP).

"On a Sabbath Jesus was teaching in one of the synagogues, and a woman was there who had been crippled by a spirit for eighteen years. She was bent over and could not straighten up at all. When Jesus saw her, "Woman, you are set free from your infirmity." Then he put his hands on her, and immediately she straightened up and praised God."

"He replied, 'Because you have so little faith. Truly I tell you, if you have faith as small as a mustard seed, you can say to this mountain, "Move from here to there," and it will move. Nothing will be impossible for you'" (Matthew 17:20).

Spiritual Warfare—Fighting Back

A prayer for wholeness and healing:

I ask you, Lord, to replace every seed of infirmity with your salvation, giving me wholeness in every area of my life! I do not say I have "inherited" sickness or disease; rather I declare "no weapon of sickness or disease" will succeed against my physical body for any reason whatsoever! I invite the Spirit of almighty God into my home afresh today. I declare his health and healing will prevail in my life and the lives of every member of my family!

In Jesus's name, I ask that you make all things new in my life right now. What lies am I believing about healing?

- *What in my body is not healed? Ask Holy Spirit to show you. Pray this statement Make my body new and help me to cooperate with you in every way. Make my mindset new and fill me with love, joy, peace, and faithfulness.*

   What mindset shift needs to take place? Ask God to give you wisdom, guidance, direction, and strategy from heaven that only you can give. Fill me with your fresh wind, fresh vision, fresh anointing, and fresh fire.

- *Ask Holy Spirit to show you where you need motivation and inspiration to start afresh. Give me inspiration, motivation, and desire again. Please help me and fill*

me up with your strength and anointing.

- *What is blocking the Holy Spirit from flowing in your*

   life? I ask in Jesus's name that you would also fill me

   with your prophetic flow. Fill me with your Spirit of

   prophecy and help me to operate in all the gifts you

   have given me.

- *Ask Holy Spirit to cleanse the spirit of negativity and*

   wash away every bitterness from your heart.

Lie #3: God Doesn't See Me

"Lack and need—if you will double down and GET
FOCUSED on what I want you to do, not getting
distracted by everything else that calls your name.
Time with me; time with your family, peace and
rest; quietness and solitude—all these are signs of
the abundant life. Your ability to make choices is a
manifestation of the abundant life too. I have set life
and death before you. Choose life."
—*Jamie Rohrbaugh*

So many lies clamor for our attention. Whether it's through the media, our churches, our homes, schools, or any public place, we are always subject to lies. We have a directive, though, in the Bible: to speak truth to the lies and to ask for God to whisper truths that reverse those lies. Light forces the darkness to flee and forces lies into the light. This comes back to how you see and perceive things, whether in truth or in darkness.

How Are You Fighting the Lies?

We are to learn discernment and wisdom, and those often come from life lessons. The hardest life lessons are the ones where we learn the most wisdom. When we recognize and learn from an early age that not telling the truth gets us in trouble, we can start to formulate that there are parts of life where wisdom is needed. To see that God sees us, we must be able to discern the lies which come our way. That takes time, training, and growing in the Spirit, deciding to become more like Christ even when we don't want to. It doesn't mean we give up the desires of our heart; it means we delight ourselves in Christ, and then the desires of our heart start to change to align with his desires.

Part of feeling like God doesn't see us is in the day-to-day walk of life. The Bible tells us we are sanctified and change from glory to glory, but for this to take place, we must walk out our faith realizing he does see us. It may not always feel as we think it should feel because his thoughts are not our thoughts.

Recently, Nate Johnston, author and one of the most accurate prophets today, shared a post on social media that resonated in my spirit: "I heard the Lord say, 'I have a season of conquests ahead of you but you won't be effective unless I first deliver you from the weariness and deep soul-sick discouragement you have been carrying.' He is delivering you from the mind battles, torment, and shellshock of the last season and bringing freedom to your mind, healing to your body and recovery to your soul."[2] If we walk this way, dwelling in deep disappointment, we take our gaze off Jesus and place it onto ourselves and our circumstances. This causes us to feel like God doesn't see us.

In October of 2022, the Lord said to me one Sunday morning, *"Why don't you trust me?"* And I broke down crying about what had been an unfulfilled desire of my heart. As the morning went on, the Lord highlighted 1 Chronicles 5:20: "He

---

[2] Nate Johnston, "You Are in a Season of God-Ordained Closure and Deliverance," nateandchristy.co, July 10, 2025, https://www.nateandchristy.co/prophetic-words/you-are-in-a-season-of-god-ordained-closure-deliverance.

answered their prayers, because they trusted in him." The word

trusted is related to verses Isaiah 26:3—"You will keep in perfect

peace those whose minds are steadfast, because they trust in

you"—and Psalm 26:1 (NLT)—"Declare me innocent, O LORD,

for I have acted with integrity; I have trusted in the LORD without

wavering."

Are we trusting him amid feeling like he doesn't see us?

And if we don't trust him, how will that take us away from seeing

his hand in our life entirely? As I pondered how much the Father

was chasing me, trying to get my attention, he brought up the

phrase "daughter of Zion." Through a friend, he said, go look up

"daughter of Zion" in the Bible. Then I saw this in *Crosswalk*, a

devotional and online resource tool: "I wonder, if as a Daughter of

Zion, I truly recognize God's intense love for me; that I'm his, and

thus, protected from the enemy. I'm a daughter emerging from the

promise God to his people; that he would provide a Savior for everyone who calls on his name for salvation."[3] If we would just ask him to drop the scales from our eyes and see how he sees, we would see how beautiful his love is for us. He wants to show us how he sees us and others. So when you feel like your prayers aren't being answered or even heard, or like you've hit the glass ceiling in life, look up. Ask to be given a bigger vision, greater wisdom, so you can peer into the Father's heart of love.

Your Personal Choices Have Eternal Consequences

When we believe God doesn't see us, we act out of lack. We strive to get our needs met outside God and his provision. What we can't see happening in the natural world, we try to fill through our own desires and choices. This comes back to coming into alignment with the Holy Spirit and saying, "Lord, will you help me to be obedient?" It comes back to surrender and love. Love is an action, and it causes us to act on behalf of God or

---

[3] Candice Lucey, "Why Christians Should Understand the Daughter of Zion," Crosswalk.com, November 10, 2020, https://www.crosswalk.com/faith/bible-study/why-christians-should-understand-the-daughter-of-zion.html.

ourselves. Surrendering can be easy or hard. When we stop being double-minded and begin to focus on the Lord and his will for our life, surrender becomes easier.

The Truth: God Sees Me

Hagar is an example in the Bible of someone who felt unseen and unloved. The maidservant to Abraham's wife, Sarah, she was basically "used" to help God bring forth the promise given to Abraham and Sarah of seeing many generations come to pass (like the stars in the sky). Can you imagine being a slave and being told whom to sleep with and when? Sex trafficking like this is common in today's world, and it's been going on for thousands of years. However, God redeems. After Hagar gave birth to Abraham's son, Ishmael, Sarah told Abraham to get rid of Hagar and the boy, and they fled into the wilderness. Hagar was crying in the desert, desperate because she believed they would die without water. An angel of the Lord showed up and said to Hagar, "What is the matter, Hagar? Do not be afraid; God had heard the boy crying as he lies there" (Genesis 21:17). And the Lord prophesied over Ishmael that he would become the father of many nations too. Just like with Hagar, when we are at our lowest and believe that the Lord doesn't see us, that is when miracles start to take place. God lifted Hagar's head, gave her a vision of water nearby, and helped her and Ishmael live.

God sees us. The Bible tells us he numbered the hairs on our head and the days of our life are written in the Book of Life. He birthed us from our mother's womb and brought us into the world. In our choices we either choose him or walk away to another destination. As our Father, it must pain him when we choose not to follow him. He imagined us into being. He created us to know him and be with him daily. He knows when we sit down and when we rise and is familiar with all our ways. We don't have to shy away from him in shame because of sin; we can come to him in humility and surrender and let him know when we need his help. Resting in his love frees us to walk with him daily. God wants to show you how much he sees you and to prophesy over your life your purpose.

Scripture Verses About God Seeing Us

Hagar in Genesis

Hagar felt abandoned and alone in the wilderness. She obeyed her master, Abraham, and left when told. Little did she know what God would do through her son, and he saw her. He met her in the wilderness to comfort and prophesy over her.

"God heard the boy crying, and the angel of God called to Hagar from heaven and said to her, 'What is the matter, Hagar? Do not be afraid; God has heard the boy crying as he lies there. Lift the boy up and take him by the hand, for I will make him into a great nation.' Then God opened her eyes and she saw a well of water. So she went and filled the skin with water and gave the boy a drink. God was with the boy as he grew up. He lived in the desert and became an archer. While he was living in the Desert of Paran, his mother got a wife for him from Egypt" (Genesis 21:17–21).

Psalm 139 (from Father's Love Letter)

My Child, you may not know everything about me, but I know everything about you. PSALM 139:1 I know when you sit down and when you rise up. PSALM 139:2 I am familiar with all your ways. PSALM 139:3 Even the very hairs on your head are numbered. MATTHEW 10:29–31 For you were made in my image. GENESIS 1:27 In my you move and have your being. For you are my offspring ACTS 17:28 I knew you before you were even conceived. JEREMIAH 1:4–5 I chose you when I planned creation EPHESIANS 1:11–12 You were not a mistake for all your days are written in my book. PSALM 139:15–16[4]

Spiritual Warfare—Fighting Back

1. He's calling us to stand from a stance of victory. Where do you see him showing you that he sees you?

---

[4] "Father's Love Letter: An Intimate Message from God to You," FathersLoveLetter.com, accessed November 17, 2025, file:///Users/deb/Downloads/Fathers-Love-Letter.pdf.

2. How can you let Psalm 139 permeate you to the depths of your being?

How can you advance the kingdom? When you know God sees you, you can take your place in the kingdom army God is building. As I once shared in a talk I gave, "We're advancing the front lines. This is a time to rise and stand . . . keep standing. Do not listen to fear or lies. Just keep standing. You are a warrior bride! Declare his Word over your life, over your situation and circumstances, over the nations. Never back down when you get battle weary; other believers will come alongside you and hold you up, just as there will be times you hold others up. Surround yourself with kingdom-minded people and with other warriors."

Prayer

Lord, help us to know and understand the depth to which you see us. To know in our bones that you died to save us all from destruction and to bring us into right standing with you. Thank you for seeing us and loving us even when we don't know the end of our sometimes difficult circumstances. You are a marvelous and

amazing God, and we long to see your kingdom come to the earth!

Lie #4: God Doesn't Care

"Reject the lies and the failure, and ask yourself;
who is fighting for you? Who wages war with you?
Who is by your side? Who will never let you do this
alone? That's right, I am with you."
—*Nate Johnston*

In February 2021, I had a conversation with a new
acquaintance I had met after a church service. Michelle said, "A
great lie from people and the pit of hell is the need to stay in
marriage for the kids. People value the institution over the
individual." As I pondered this lie, the Lord said, "I no longer want
to see you trampled on, abused, put down, and led astray. I want
you to be free to chase after me." He values people so much he
chases after them as well, which shows us our beauty and worth.
We are so valuable to his kingdom. Hearing a contradictory
statement to what is preached in Western churches, that divorce is
a sin, threw me for a loop. How long had I believed this lie of
staying married for the kids? As I untangled this next phase of lies

in my life, it became clear I was believing the lie that God doesn't care. Why would a big God care about someone as insignificant as me? The truth is, though, he loves us so much, he died on a cross to save us. No other God in history has accomplished the biggest miracle of all time.

Another lie I've believed is that I was not worthy enough to be loved, so why would God care about me? Unmet needs caused me to search out love in places and in people I shouldn't have. These places and people weren't wrong; they just weren't God's best for me. If I loved myself as we are told to in Matthew and Deuteronomy, wouldn't that cause others to love me too? Not always. Walking through a season of learning to love myself despite my past and pedigree brought about transformation in both my physical self and my spiritual self. God knew how to grow me, and it was through the very hard lesson of recognizing my unmet needs and finding healthy ways to get those needs satisfied.

What if someone saw below the surface and had the courage to help me meet those needs? That would be a great gift from God. I believed for so long that wasn't possible. I told myself no one wanted to get to know the real me, cherish me, protect me, or protect my heart, lift me up, or encourage me to keep going. It was all about sacrificing myself to meet the needs of others. That's not compassion. That's not being loving toward myself. I want to get to know others for who they really are.

Coming out from under this season really had me on a mission to figure out not only how I played a part in the destruction of my own story through thoughts, choices, and lies but to understand how many lies have been taught to us in the Western church. I began searching out biblical Hebrew and Greek meanings to words like submission, leadership, marriage, covenant, and lies. When God sends you on a word search, you listen and dig. Digging into the Word of God is one of the most beneficial ways to grow in relationship with him. As I dug into these words, trying to tackle this huge task of understanding where I was taught different meanings, I came to understand what real love and relationships look like with our Creator and other people. I also came to understand that God does care for me. The divorce season I had walked through was so difficult (don't wish it on anyone) but one of the most merciful seasons of his grace. God also showed me where there are biblical reasons for divorce and where there are not. He cared enough to come down into my story and rewrite it for my good and the good of my children.

Biblical Reason for Divorce

Patrick Weaver states,

Divorce does not cause someone to commit adultery if they divorce based on biblical grounds. The biblical grounds for divorce have rarely been taught truthfully or accurately by religion, particularly toxic religion. Jesus's statement about committing adultery if someone remarries is related to someone leaving a covenant marriage for no reason at all except to fulfill the lust of the flesh. Jesus was talking to religious men who were throwing their wives away to be with other women. In the Bible, men were responsible for divorcing their wives because women were unable to divorce their husbands since they were considered property and not equal under the law. Jesus came to fulfill the law and set the captives free, which included the slave-like relationship between a woman and her husband (Galatians 3:28).

A woman can divorce an unrepentant and abusive man for biblical reasons: adultery or perverseness, or abandonment, whether physical or behavioral. Divorce based on biblical grounds nullifies the marriage and sets the injured spouse free according to God's will and plan for their life (Jeremiah 29:11).

The divorced can remarry because their marriage was nullified by covenant violation. The biblical teaching that reports otherwise is false teaching.

Divorce and Abuse—Untangling the Lies

When you project others' behavior and what they have done to you onto God, you believe the lie that God doesn't care. Why would he allow such misery and misuse of his Word? He doesn't like misbehavior, but the thing is we as humans have free will. We have free will to choose how to treat others. Will we treat them with dignity or respect? Or will we use them to satisfy our own needs? When we step outside his will and mistreat others, the result can be abuse in many situations.

Abuse comes in many different forms. So many people stay in relationships with people who are abusive, whether it's spiritual, emotional, psychological, verbal, financial, sexual, or physical abuse. Many people don't even understand they are being abused. Because of the lies perpetuated toward us by the enemy, we need to take the time to untangle the words and lies that keep us in bondage while being abused.

The Truth: God Does Care

Thinking God doesn't care or see our situation causes us to step away from God. We must stay grounded in his Word, in prayer, and in time spent at his feet. Ask God to show you where he was during the hard times. He will show you how he was with you in each of those hard situations. And each lie you've believed by you, he will untangle if you let him. In these intimate moments with him, he will show you where he was during each step of that untangling process. Inner healing gets to the root cause of each lie told to us or agreement we've come into with, with the enemy. In turn, God will show us how much he cares; he wants to unearth the lies so you can live an abundant life. A life of daily surrender and sacrifice and dependence on him will move mountains.

The thing is God does care. He cares more than we realize. Isaiah 46:4 (GNT) says, "I am your God and will take care of you until you are old and your hair is gray. I made you and will care for you." He cares about the tiniest things, and when we start to recognize that those "lucky things" are not coincidences but God saying hi, we wake up to so many fun surprises he has in store.

Let me share an example. I really wanted a weighted vest for my birthday and needed to spend my birthday money on clothes. But God saw this sweet tiny desire in my life and provided a $100 Amazon gift card at an event I went to. I was elated and went straight to Amazon and bought the weighted vest. It's not always about *things*, but sometimes God does reach down if we are paying attention, and he does so to show us he cares. It's in both the tiny things and the big things that we start to realize there is a God who sees us. I love the verse in Isaiah telling us God will take care of us until we are old and gray. He created us to live an abundant life, filled with his power and love so we can help others and bring them into the kingdom.

He sees you, beloved, and loves you more than you can measure.

Scripture Verses About God's Concern for Us

"I will sing a new song to you . . . to the One who gives victory to kings, who delivers his servant David" (Psalm 144:9–10).

"Do not be afraid or discouraged because of this vast army. For the battle is not yours, but God's" (2 Chronicles 20:15).

"You can be sure that God will take care of everything you need, his generosity exceedingly even yours in the glory that pours from Jesus" (Philippians 4:19 MSG).

"I am your God and will take care of you until you are old and your hair is gray" (Isaiah 46:4 GNT).

"He will not allow your foot to slip; He who keeps you will not slumber" (Psalm 121:3 AMP).

"Jesus said, 'Father, forgive them, for they do not know what they are doing.' And they divided up his clothes by casting lots" (Luke 23:34).

Spiritual Warfare—Fighting Back

The enemy's agenda is destruction, and his strategy is division. Unforgiveness is a foothold for the enemy—you can't kick out the enemy if you're leaving the door open.

When someone offends you, go to them. On the other side of forgiveness is the peace you are looking to find. Revenge kills you more than the person who hurt you. Forgiveness is the only way. God cares too much to leave you in unforgiveness towards anyone. Anytime you experience heartache or grief in relationships, it's important to cleanse the footholds and not allow forgiveness to take root. That can cause all kinds of issues to enter into your life and not allow you to walk forward into freedom. When you need to be forgiven, follow these helpful steps:

1. Recognize your wrongdoing.

2. Repent with genuine remorse.

3. Walk in understanding and grace if they don't respond the way you hope.

4. Work on rebuilding trust and repairing the damage you caused.

5. Daily choose to receive and release God's forgiveness.

6. Ask yourself, *What do I need to grow in today? Where am I supposed to forgive? Where have I missed something?*

5 Common Rationalizations for Not Forgiving Someone Else

1. "Can't forgive; it's too big." The bigger it is, you don't want to carry it. Time to let it go!

2. "People say I can't forgive, and time will heal it." Time can't heal it.

3. "I'll forgive them when they say they're sorry!"

4. "I can't forgive If I can't forget."

5. "I can't forgive them because they will do it again."

What is meant for harm God uses for good. In Genesis 50:20 Joseph reminds us what is possible when forgiveness is all we have.

How to Forgive

1. Decide to forgive.

2. Depend on the Holy Spirit.

3. Prayer and ask the Lord to show you what needs to be forgiven.

4. Obey and listen. Listen to the Lord and listen to the other person's point of view.

Prayer:

This morning I'm thankful that I can begin my day just sitting in your presence, resting at your feet. As the world around me swirls with fear, uncertainty, and chaos, I am very grateful that you are

my constant refuge. It is reassuring to me that you always know

what is weighing on my heart and filling up my mind before I even

speak a word. Thank you that I can be still with you, and you will

bless me with the strength, peace, and perseverance to go into this

day ahead. As I close my eyes and breathe, let me feel your Spirit

that is within me. Let it be the guiding force that directs my steps

this day. In the name of Jesus, amen!

Lie #5: God Doesn't Perform Miracles

"If I was living in the advantage Jesus describes, I
would want less."
—Bill Johnson

God is the God of miracles. He wants to show us so many
things our minds can't even begin to comprehend. We as a body of
Christ have given up on seeing the miraculous. Many
denominations believe miracles ceased after the Bible was written.
As you explore church history, that could not be further from the
truth. Looking at revivals and revival history, you begin to see how
miracles have been a part of history over time. The miraculous has
flowed through different movements, people, and places. People in
Western culture are some of the sickest in the world. This is due to
multiple factors, such as limited access to clean drinking water,
diet, lifestyle, etc., but there is often a cure. And God doesn't just
perform miracles in people's health. The miraculous can happen in
all areas of life. Can we cultivate a culture where we expect the

miraculous? Where hope abounds? Where can we pray to see his glory invade the world and our homes? Let us come out from under the lie that miracles don't happen today.

As I have deconstructed after being raised cessationist (the belief that the gifts of the Spirit, as referenced in 1 Corinthians 12, are no longer active in the church today) and have started to walk more in line with the Holy Spirit, it has become apparent I had believed the lie that God doesn't perform miracles. I thought miracles only happened in the Bible but weren't for today—especially after walking through one of the hardest seasons of my life where we lost three babies. I could have dealt with all those traumas and wounds in a healthier way by going to God and the Holy Spirit first and then going to doctors. I searched and searched for answers, but they didn't come in the natural as I hoped. I would find one answer of needing to be gluten-free, not realizing that most auto-immune disease is rooted in trauma and can be healed from the ground up. Then, I encountered the miraculous when I had my two children. They are walking, talking miracles, and I'm delighted to be their mother. I use this story to showcase the lies we come into agreement with that keep us hindered and in sin, unable to walk out the supernatural abundance he supplies us every day.

More Excellent Way in Health

One of my counselors recommended the book *A More Excellent Way, Be in Health* by Dr. Henry Wright. It is a fascinating read in which he claims that 80 percent of all diseases are rooted in trauma and unforgiveness.[5] The beginning of all healing of spiritually rooted diseases begins when you make your peace with God and accept his love once and for all, accepting yourself and accepting others. Dr. Wright states,

'Would you consider fear to be sin?

Would you consider bitterness to be a sin?

Would you consider self-hatred to be sin?
The word says they are.

---

[5] Henry Wright, *A More Excellent Way, Be in Health: Spiritual Roots of Disease, Pathways to Wholeness* (Whitaker House, 2009), 261.

A virus has an intelligence behind it that defies imagination. Attacking it as spirits of infirmity. Jesus cast out spirits of infirmity with His words. Is it released because of another spiritual problem called fear, anxiety, and stress?

We can open the doors to sin, and we close the doors by resisting the enemy. Addiction, alcoholism, sexual perversion, narcissism, anger, abuse, rape, molestation, fear, greed, racism, religion, and idolatry are a few examples.[6]

When we open the doors to sin, we must face the reality that we've opened the doors to different sicknesses as a result of sin. When we repent, we cancel the ability for sin to torment us, and we turn and walk away from it. By walking and continuing to walk with a forgiving heart, we can walk into further freedom and resist the enemy.

---

[6] Henry Wright, *A More Excellent Way, Be in Health: Spiritual Roots of Disease, Pathways to Wholeness* (Whitaker House, 2009), 8.

Generational Curses

Resist the enemy and take out generational curses. When we believe a lie, we give legal rights to the enemy to enter in. This lie can go up and down the family line, unnecessarily causing torment to not only yourself but those in your family. This causes sin to enter our lives, and it can allow the enemy to torment us; it is all canceled by repentance. Don't allow the lie to invade the family line causing torment unnecessarily in your family. As Isaiah 33:22 says, "For the LORD is our judge, the LORD is our lawgiver, the LORD is our king; it is he who will save us." Genesis 12:2–3 (NASB) also tells us that "in you [Abraham] all the families of the earth will be blessed."

Generational blessings come through our faith in God and his Word. In Matthew 4, Jesus used the Word to resist temptation. Generational blessings are possible today, and it comes through teaching repentance from sin when we act out selfishly as children and also showing our kids that the love of God and accepting him as savior cancels our debts.

Take the following verses as confirmation about what God says about the generations and how important it is to walk uprightly with the Lord in order see his favor multiple toward your family. Psalm 112:1–2 says, "The generation of the upright will be blessed." Proverbs 20:7 (CSB) says, "A righteous person acts with integrity; his children who came after him will be happy." Jeremiah 32:8 (CSB) says, "You show faithful love to thousands but lay the fathers' iniquity on their sons' laps after them, great and mighty God whose name is the LORD of Armies."

Generational blessings will flow when we come into agreement with God's words and live them out in our daily walk with Jesus. You can be the bondage breaker in your family line, paving the way for blessings for future generations.

How Healing and Deliverance Together Create the Miraculous and Mysterious

My friend Dana Lyn shared these wise words with me once:

In this ministry, we assume it is always God's will to heal because he instructed us to do so. He gave us authority over the enemy and to heal every disease and sickness. He instructed us to lay hands on the sick and there is a promise that the prayers and acts of faith will bring healing. When Jesus died, "He took up our infirmities and bore our diseases" and it was declared in Isaiah that "with his stripes we are healed." In 2 Corinthians 12:7–10. The accuser could have come before the Lord to accuse Paul of pride and boasting. God could have allowed that demon to torment him to ensure that he stays humble to continue to do the great exploits of the Lord in His strength and not His own.

There are times when God's purposes go beyond our human comprehension, and He does things for His will and His good pleasure that we may not understand. In Job we learn that the enemy can't do anything without God's permission. God allowed Satan to torment Job, a righteous man who didn't sin. Suffering does not automatically mean someone is receiving Gods' punishment. The examples of Job as well as John 9:3 below, we see that there was no sin, but it was that God's works would be displayed in his life. We see in Matthew 17 and Luke 8 below how faith is linked to receiving healing as well as the ability to drive out devils. So, we assume that is always God's will to heal, and if the healing doesn't come there is a legal right for the enemy to torment, or it is God's will and purpose for something else to be accomplished through that suffering. Sometimes the enemy is hiding behind the wounded soul, lies the person believes, their open doors to sin, etc.

Sometimes it is simply a mystery of God and we lean not on our own understanding.[7]

The Truth: God Performs Miracles

I had the privilege of meeting with a minister named Chuck. Chuck had been in healing ministries within the Methodist Church for a long time and had learned from Randy Clark, founder of Global Awakening and author of several books on the topic of healing. His stories were nothing short of miraculous. He asked us if he could tell a story, and we said sure. He proceeded to tell us

---

[7] Dana Lyn, text message to the author, August 2025.

about some of their best friends and their daughter-in-law who in her early twenties was about to be rushed to Oklahoma City because her heart was failing and needed a heart transplant. Her heart was functioning at 19 percent. So Chuck prayed with his friend, and while he was on the phone praying, he fell asleep. This happened once, twice, and then a third time. Chuck was so embarrassed. While he was praying on the phone with his friend, her heart stabilized enough that they didn't need to rush her to OKC. The next day, he went to the ICU to pray over her because she was still being monitored before they were going to transfer her with his friend and their family. As he prayed over her, he started praying in tongues. Realizing what he had done, he stopped and apologized for not asking permission first. He then asked if he could pray in tongues and said he always asks permission, and everyone agreed. While he was praying for her, her heart function rose to 50 percent. The next day or a few days after, he visited her one more time as she had been transferred out of ICU and onto a different floor. Her heart had stabilized but was nowhere near 100 percent. He went into her room, and she told him what was going on, and he looked at her and said, "Let's get this heart completely healed." He told her to keep her eyes open, to pray in agreement, and they would get her heart to 100 percent. And that's exactly what happened. Today she is alive and healthy!

The funny thing about this story was that every time Chuck fell asleep while praying with his friend on the phone, he was actually going into praying in tongues. Chuck said sometimes the Holy Spirit has to get you out of the way in order to use you. Chuck's faith was mind blowing and a walking testimony of what God can do through faithful obedience if we just say yes.

Scripture Verses About Miracles

"This was to fulfill what was spoken through the prophet Isaiah: 'He took up our infirmities and bore our diseases'" (Matthew 8:17).

"Jesus called his twelve disciples to him and gave them authority to drive out impure spirits and to heal every disease and sickness" (Matthew 10:1).

"They shall lay hands on the sick, and they shall recover" (Mark 16:18 KJV).

"Is anyone among you sick? Let them call the elders of the church to pray over them and anoint them with oil in the name of the Lord. And the prayer offered in faith will make the sick person well; the Lord will raise them up. If they have sinned, they will be forgiven" (James 5:14–15).

"'Neither this man nor his parents sinned,' said Jesus, 'but this happened so that the works of God might be displayed in him.'" (John 9:3).

"Jesus rebuked the demon, and it came out of the boy, and he was healed at that moment. Then the disciples came to Jesus in private and asked, 'Why couldn't we drive it out?' He replied, 'Because you have so little faith. Truly I tell you, if you have faith as small as a mustard seed, you can say to this mountain, "Move from here to there," and it will move. Nothing will be impossible for you'" (Matthew 17:18–20).

"And a woman was there who had been subject to bleeding for twelve years, but no one could heal her. She came up behind him and touched the edge of his cloak, and immediately her bleeding stopped. . . . Then he said to hear, 'Daughter, your faith has healed you. Go in peace'" Luke 8:43–44, 48).

Spiritual Warfare—Fighting Back

A prayer for breaking generational curses (from Kristy Wentz with Finding Freedom Ministries):

Lord, right now I ask that all the sins of my fathers and forefathers and every attached curse be bought before You. We know that the blood of Your Son covers every sin and turns every curse into a blessing. Lord, I confess and denounce the sings of my ancestors, and ask that You apply the blood of Your Son to every sin and curse that may be in my lineage or on my life. Father, thank you for

forgiving these sins and separating me from these curses. Amen.

Prayer

Holy Spirit, help get me out of the way and bring this miracle to

your feet. We ask that you show us each day who to pray for and

how to pray for them. We want to walk in your authority and power

to trample on serpents and bring about your glory to the world.

May you heed our prayers for miracles and meet us in the messy

middle. We are in awe of you and pray for your miracles to invade

our world.

Lie #6: God Isn't Real

"The storm doesn't define you, it reveals who you
are really are."
—*Sammy Rodriguez*

The year 2020 was a wasteland for so many. At times, even though the Lord had brought me through so much, I wondered if he was real, considering what was going on in my life. The day I signed my divorce papers, the Lord said to my heart, *"I'm speaking over many daughters of God. The enemy may have thought he could touch and steal your voice, but I say unto you, I am now amplifying my voice through you."* It was the birthing of something new. New is hard, though, especially after grief. We wonder what it's like to move forward, in the pain. Is he there? Is he really letting this happen? During this season of wrestling, the Lord kept bringing up the word *untangle*. This led me to find an article by Gerrie Bester on untangling with a deeper look at Matthew 19:24:

The picture, the Hebrew context of this scripture paints is as follows: You have to loosen or untangle yourself from that which the world wants to bind you with. The moment you untangle yourself from that which is carnal and material and seek the presence of God you can build a covenant relationship with Him. The rich young man wanted to do all the deeds of obedience but was not willing to put Abba Father in the rightful place in his life. Jesus wanted the young man to untangle his heart from material things and seek Abba Father. When you seek the "stuff" you miss the Source of provision, Abba Father. Jesus wanted to turn his heart to the Father and get him to loosen his reliance on his "purse." Seek first the Kingdom of God and His righteousness, and all these things shall be added unto you (Matthew 6:33)[8]

The definition of *untangle* is to free from a tangle, to disentangle. The synonym is to extricate. To straighten out, clarify,

---

[8] Gerrie Bester, "Untangle yourself," Facebook post, Prof Gerrie Bester – Roaring Truth Ministries's Post, June 4, 2020, https://www.facebook.com/ProfGerrieBester/posts/untangle-yourself-in-matthew-19-you-read-about-a-rich-young-man-this-rich-young-/686241108614057/.

or resolve. To loose from tangle or intricacy; hence, to free from embarrassment, doubt or uncertainty, resolve, clear up; explain. Untangle suggests the painstaking separation of a thing from other things. This means to be freed from what binds or holds back.

The thing was, I couldn't keep all the plates in my life spinning—my marriage, playing victim, and caring about what others thought. The other point was other people didn't see God in the whole process. The Lord was extricating me from a relationship, and nobody understood what was truly going on below the surface in each of our lives. At the end of the day, relationships have two people who have margin for each other. Both people have their own stuff they bring into the relationship. And it's up to each person to untangle their stuff, desire and choose to own it, and repent—that is, in a healthy relationship.

Why did I accept anything less and tolerate the constant neglect? Why did I project onto God the lie that he wasn't real because he wasn't stopping the hardship? Untangling the lies is a process of coming into our wholeness; if you know your identity, the less likely you are to accept behaviors and false hopes that keep you bound. We all have these beliefs and frameworks that we have to walk out. Now I am less likely than before to tolerate what is unhealthy. My ex-husband was emotionally neglecting his family, and when that dynamic exists, the guilty spouse will often test to see how far they can neglect and how long their spouse will remain. If you're being neglected in this way, you must figure out why you allow these people to enter your front door. It's easy to get married, but be careful to be equally yoked. Certain people in the Bible were molded by God to be consistent in their nature. God brings our biblical heroes out of life-altering situations, and everyone knew God was their God. For example, Joseph had the mark of God on his life. He grew through hardship and came to know God is real. Look at the end of Genesis, where Joseph tells his brothers, "You intended to harm me, but God intended it for good to accomplish what is now being done, the saving of many lives" (Genesis 50:20). You don't get to that place of acceptance unless you know God is real and you have an inheritance in Christ.

In Christ, we each have an inheritance. Ephesians 1:18 (AMP) says, "And [I pray] that the eyes of your heart [the very center and core of your being] may be enlightened [flooded with light by the Holy Spirit], so that you will know and cherish the hope [the divine guarantee, the confident expectation] to which He has called you, the riches of His glorious inheritance in the saints (God's people)." From the book *The Threshold*, we learn that "God has incredible plans and purposes for your life. He desires to do so much in you and through you. The devil can't take those plans and purposes away. But we can give them up. God gave us appetites and desires. They are good. They're part of being human. But we are responsible for how we use and direct them."[9] If we can grasp our inheritance, untangle the lies and yokes of the enemy, we can run forward with fervor and strength. We can steward our lives, in partnership with the Holy Spirit, to say, "God, you are real. You are more real than the sunrise and the sunset. You

---

[9] Craig Cooney, *The Threshold: 50 Days of Prophetic Keys and Biblical Insights for Crossing Over* (pub. by author, 2024), page#?.

breathe life into our beings and lungs, and you desire to heal our hearts this side of heaven."

Let him untangle your heart. Let him breathe new life into your being. He is so real and desires to show you each day how much he loves you regardless of your choices and the lies you believe in. He is that good.

The Truth: God Is Real

Where do you begin with believing that God is real? In the beginning God created the heavens and the earth (Genesis 1:1). If that is true, then there is a God behind everything you see. There are two worlds at play: the natural and the supernatural. Most people don't even begin to comprehend how much more there is to the bigger story of creation, the creation both of humans and of supernatural beings. We can learn so much about this from Michael Heiser in his book *The Unseen Realm*. That story is too big to go into here, but if you decide to read that book, you will recognize the complexity of the Bible and how the creation story didn't just come into being spontaneously. It was created by a supernatural God who miraculously lives in you when you accept him as Lord and Savior. As the Lord says in Revelation 22:13, "I am the Alpha and the Omega, the First and the Last, the Beginning and the End." Let that sink in. The Alpha and Omega is real and lives inside you. When you look around and marvel at the beauty in this world, remember there is a big God who created you and wants to be with you every day.

As you wrestle with the truth of God being real, remember this is a love story. One created outside time and space, one where an infinite God didn't want to live without you. He walked across this time and space continuum only to discover that he was writing a love story meant to be played out in each individual's life.

Scripture Verses About the Reality of God

"God is not human, that he should lie" (Numbers 23:19).

"The heavens declare the glory of God; the skies proclaim the work of his hands" (Psalm 19:1).

"For in him all things were created: things in heaven and on earth, visible and invisible, whether thrones or powers or rulers or authorities; all things have been created through him and for him" (Colossians 1:16).

"But because of his great love for us, God, who is rich in mercy, made us alive with Christ even when we were dead in transgressions—it is by grace you have been saved" (Ephesians 2:4–5).

Spiritual Warfare—Fighting Back

1. How is God showing you he is real? Ask him to show up in your dreams, through people, signs and wonders, miracles, and in his Word.

2. How can you be reflective and repentant for the times you received Jesus with joy but then, in trials, rejected him as King and Lord in your life?

3. Pray for help to stay in steadfast love and commitment to the Lord in your life and in the body of Christ. We should be devoted to his heart and ways in all we do.

Prayer

Your love for each person is so great, filled with green pastures and life. Thank you that you go before us and behind us. You provide rest and lay down everything in front of us, helping us to laugh, celebrate, and even grieve. You help us to walk forward in the next season. You see history as a book of pages, so, Lord, protect us and give us discernment. Our arms are wide open as we speak visions, but help us not be bound within them. Give us freedom, and let the path fulfill the words given by God.

Lie #7: Satan Isn't Real

"The finest trick of the devil is to persuade you that
he does not exist."
—Charles Baudelaire

I can look back now on many times where darkness had been present, where different lies I believed kept me entangled in sin and not seeking righteousness. Some large lies and some smaller ones. We should never give too much credence to darkness, because Jesus said, "Take heart; I have overcome the world" (John 16:33 ESV), and "You, dear children, are from God and have overcome them, because the one who is in you is greater than the one who is in the world" (1 John 4:4). We are not to fear the enemy, but we are to understand we have an enemy and he seeks to destroy our lives. That's why it's so important to know who you are and whose you are.

Recently I was walking on the beach, doing something I love to do, which is pick up seashells and collect them. The Lord said to my heart, *"They are unique like snowflakes, and this is the way I've made you—unique."* I have a seashell collection from all the beaches around the world that I have visited over the years. Each unique seashells represents a different part of the world. I marvel at God's creation—whether it's sunrises, sunsets, mountains, beaches, or all the amazing people he's created. When I meet someone who isn't walking with the Lord or doesn't know God, it hurts my heart. You can see their story etched on their face and in their eyes. I always wonder, *What lie do you believe that keeps you from God's goodness? What dark thing have you faced and let win in your life?* I believe God loves each of us and we get to choose: him or not him. It's a very simple choice with lifelong and eternal consequences. But for some people, it comes with seasons of wrestling in the darkness. The darkness wins when we don't understand the lie that Satan isn't real. He is very real, but take heart, for God has overcome the world.

When God calls you forward, don't look back. When he says to walk out of the grave, take off those grave clothes, and choose to walk with him—do it! The article below from Steve

Porter really helps explain how to put the past behind us, trampling

on the enemy and moving forward in life from this lie.

Five Things We Should Never Look Back On[10]

1. **The Sin God Saved You From (Think of Lot's Wife)**

   The sins of this world have nothing to offer, and neither

   does a shallow, empty, lukewarm and carnal life. . . .

   The Father's greatest desire is for your life to reflect

   His holiness and glory and not end in shame or

   disgrace. Therefore, He commands us to set our faces

   like flints, with a fierce and relentless determination to

   do His will and to live according to our destiny. . . .

2. **Your Past Sins and Failures**

   . . . (Philippians 3:13–14). Here Paul was saying, *I'm*

   not there yet. . . . But one thing is for sure: it's time to

---

[10] The five sections below are excerpted from Steve Porter, "When God Calls You Forward, Don't Look Back," The Elijah List, ElijahList.com, August 20, 2022, https://www.elijahlist.com/words/display_word.html?ID=27851.

stop focusing on the past and start reaching out to

finish our race, winning souls while there's still time!

It's easy to dwell on things we can't change, but when

we do that, we're no longer able to step forward and

follow the Spirits lead, accomplishing our next

assignments as unto the Lord. Satan's goal is for us to

be haunted, distracted, and powerless to move forward;

he wants us to spend the rest of our days wearing rags

and begging for the love God has already displayed so

beautifully. . . . We must get excited, knowing the best

is yet to come for those who trust in Him and walk

moment by moment according to His Word. Let's focus

on Christ and step out in obedience to our King of

kings, watching Him move in signs and wonders, just to

reveal His glory to those who need it most! . . .

3. **Missed Opportunities**

"Godly sorrow brings repentance that leads to salvation

and leaves no regret, but worldly sorrow brings death."

(2 Corinthians 7:10) . . . God is raising up a Bride who will stop mourning and instead run after Him to receive the new opportunities He has for them. It's time to shed those grave clothes, because it's going to be glorious!

4. **Past Pain and Hurt**

"I will repay you for the years the locus have eaten— the great locust and the young locust, the other locusts and the locus swarm—My great army I sent among you." (Joel 2:25) . . . Scripture promises that our God is God of restoration! He will restore all that the locusts have eaten in our lives, if we will refuse to hold on to pain, bitterness and resentment, and allow Him to heal our hearts and restore us.

5. **The Former Things**

"Forget the former things; do not dwell on the past. See, I am doing a new thing! Now it springs up; do you not perceive it? I am making a way in the wilderness and streams in the wasteland." (Isaiah 43:18–19) . . . to hunger and thirst for a fresh move of God. . . . We must

be careful not to get stuck in past moves, miracles and

manifestations. We must ask Him for a fresh wave of

His Spirit to usher in great and mighty things He wants

to do now. . . .

The Bride of Christ must not look back but instead look

forward with great anticipation for God is doing in this

hour. In this moment, let's be alert and on guard,

walking in harmony with God's Spirit to win the prize.

The Truth: Satan Is Real

A friend of mine is a survivor of satanic ritual abuse, or

SRA as it's abbreviated. When she first told me her story, I was

blown away. I had heard of satanic sacrifices at Halloween, but

beyond that I didn't understand the depth to which the satanic

church operates in the US (and all over the world). Her story

recounts the wild stories of animal sacrifices, being offered on the

altar to be a child sacrifice by her own mother, and the occult

trying to break into her home to scare her and her family on multiple occasions. She came to know Jesus as a teenager and broke away from her family at seventeen. What a wild story she has. But it made me realize that Satan is very real. There is a whole unseen realm that operates beyond our finite understanding. We sat down to do a deliverance at my house one day. She needed help with healing in different parts of her body. As we prayed together, the hair on my arm started to stand up. You could feel the atmosphere shift in my home, and she said, "The heavenlies are warring because they don't want to see me walk into freedom. Keep going."

In that moment, and on several other occasions around our city, God has shown me just how real the spiritual realm is. People recognize there is evil in the world, but so many Christians aren't awake to the fact that there is an enemy who prowls around trying to destroy them. Christians in the West have buried their heads in the sand. The enemy doesn't win if we believe in Jesus, but he will still try to take you out. Jesus says in John 10:10, "The thief comes only to steal and kill and destroy, but I have come that they may have life." So how do we overcome the enemy? Through the power of the blood of the lamb and the words of our testimony. Revelation 12:11 (KJV) explains, "And they overcame him by the blood of the Lamb, and by the word of their testimony; and they loved not their lives unto the death." When you accept Jesus, you are now walking in the power of the blood. His blood changes everything. Your testimony of what God has done for you will shake the chains of hell off someone's life. Sharing about God's goodness will always bring to light the darkness. We are called to walk in the light and to flee the darkness. What you put in your mind, heart, and soul will bear fruit. That fruit will either be goodness or darkness. Choose light.

Scripture Verses About the Reality of Satan

"Take heart! I have overcome the world" (John 16:33).

"You, dear children, are from God and have overcome them, because the one who is in you is greater than the one who is in the world" (1 John 4:4).

"Submit yourselves, then, to God. Resist the devil, and he will flee from you" (James 4:7).

"Be alert and of sober mind. Your enemy the devil prowls around like a roaring lion looking for someone to devour" (1 Peter 5:8). "I have given you authority to trample on snakes and scorpions and to overcome all the power of the enemy; nothing will harm you" (Luke 10:19).

Spiritual Warfare—Fighting Back

- Here's a question to consider: If you truly believe all afflictions are tied to demonic spirits and that you do not war against flesh and blood (no matter the symptoms, it's always a spirit), then what needs to shift in order to walk this out in your life? When you have authority in your spirit, then you are guaranteed victory as an expression of the spirit realm.

- What do you believe about your authority in Christ? We have power by warring prayer, intercession with prayer, and Scripture. Trampling scorpions in Scripture represents the authority of the spirit of darkness. If we are in God, our authority is in Jesus and everything has to bow to Him. When we are rightly positioned in Jesus, we must stay under him, confident in these truths, keeping our eyes on Christ so that all things not of God will fall away from us.

- The enemy will use up all our resources and money and wear us out with unnecessary resources. Ask Holy Spirit what is the first step I should take in this process? The enemy often comes in the form of sickness, and we are tempted to go down the path where sickness has power. Cleansing the footholds where the enemy has gotten in is required emotionally and spiritually, and Psalm 91 is a great scripture to help with that.

- Walking with an awareness of the spirit realm, we have the blood of Jesus on the door. No weapons formed against us can overtake us. Shield—nice try, you can't stay here. The power comes when the inner spirit comes up to the power of him. It's not about performance; we didn't have the power in our own spirit. It's in him and him alone!

- How is your intimacy with the Lord? Resisting Satan is about our relationship with God and the process he works out in us. It's also about intimacy and trusting in him. We can't get through the kingdom without dependence on Him.

Prayer

Show us, Lord, where we believe the lie that the enemy isn't real. Show us how to walk in our authority in Christ and revolt against the enemy. We have the authority to live out Luke 10:19 and to trample Satan. Help us to trample the enemy and to rise up in you!

Lie #8: Christian's Can't Be Demonically Oppressed

Jesus Himself made it plain: "And these signs will
accompany those who believe: In my name they
will drive out demons" (Mark 16:17 NIV). Who
will drive out demons? Those who believe. Not
pastors only. Not prophets. Not those with a certain
"gift." All believers.

—*Joshua Lewis*

This lie caught me by surprise when I started down my path

of freedom and healing. I had always believed that the enemy

couldn't get into our bodies and minds once saved and cause

issues. The more research and learning I did, the more I came to

understand that when we can come into agreement with lies, we

can cause evil spirits to be present.

Look at King Saul. When David played the harp, God's

Spirit would come upon him, and the evil spirit would leave.

Although this was during Old Testament days and we now have the

Holy Spirit dwelling within us, we are still at war with our heart area (body, mind, will, and emotions). But Satan cannot get enter the soul area—that is where the Holy Spirit lives in a person. The enemy can invade other areas of our life via sin, the fallen world, our choices, and even other people's choices. Matthew 12:43–45 describes this in a metaphor about a house being swept clean but the spirit comes back with seven spirits even more wicked. This passage is speaking not just about the Pharisees but about keeping our own internal 'house," or soul, clean. This means partnering with God when he shows you the little things and coming out from underneath the lie that this or that doesn't matter. One white lie or exaggeration won't matter, we think; it's just one. Next thing you know, you're like my ten-year-old grounded from Nintendo Switch because of his repeated lying. It's better to learn these lessons earlier in life than to have them on repeat causing destruction later on down the road.

One way people can come into contact with demons is through soul ties. The concept of a soul tie is not specifically defined in the Bible, but most people reference the friendship of David and Jonathan or a marital relationship as a soul tie. These are examples of healthy soul ties—being bonded to someone in a healthy way for the enrichment of each other's lives. An ungodly or unhealthy soul tie comes when there is an overdependence on a person or thing other than Jesus, making these ties hard to break. An example of this is codependency. The definition of codependency is a dysfunctional relationship dynamic where one person assumes the role of "the giver," sacrificing their own needs and well-being for the sake of the other, "the taker." The bond in question doesn't have to be romantic; it can occur just as easily between parent and child or among friends or family members.

Another way unhealthy soul ties occur is through not forgiving others and not doing the work to get free from emotional bondage. Sometimes things happen to you that are beyond your control. You cannot control another person. When you realize this and start to take action through forgiveness prayer, you start to unleash the power of God to work in your life. Below is one example of a breaking-free prayer that can unleash God to start moving and bringing freedom.

How to Overcome Ungodly Soul Ties

The following prayer from my friend and deliverance counselor, Dana Lyn, puts into perspective how to combat soul ties and break any ungodly bonds with another person causing the influence of demonic oppression.

My friend Dana Lyn says,

You say, Father God, in the name of Jesus Christ of Nazareth, I repent and renounce for me and my generations for my bitterness, unforgiveness towards another person who hurt me or manipulated or controlled me.

You say, Father God, in the name of Jesus Christ of Nazareth, I forgive myself and tear up the debt against me. I repent for participating with the fear of man, fear of rejection, co-dependency inordinate affections toward another, rejection, fear of rejection, fear of man, fear of being alone, self-pity, false burden bearing, unloving spirits, lack of trust in you, insecurity and putting expectations on another person to meet my need emotionally and to feel loved. I bind all these spirits and command all these spirits to go to dry places now in the name of Jesus Christ of Nazareth.

I now take the sword of the Spirit and cut and server all soul ties, cords, bonds and break them from me and the other person off my soul (mind, will and emotions). I take the sword of the spirit and break every tenacle or cord attached to my mind, my emotions, and my will. I declare and decree I am free. Amen.[11]

What You Think About Is What You Chase

This is where our tendencies and wiring come into play. The enemy wants to get you to step away. To step away from Jesus, from the Word, from prayer, and from godly relationships. He wants to make things look attractive and lure you to places you

---

[11] Dana Lyn, TheBlessCollective.com.

aren't supposed to go. James 1:14 (AMP) says, "But each one is tempted when he is dragged away, enticed and baited [to commit sin] by his own [worldly] desire (lust, passion)."

How does the enemy come at you? The enemy comes with a lure. His goal is to stir your affections for the sin. If you know the enemy and the battles you're in, you can work toward not getting caught up in the moment. Here are some helpful reminders:

1. Eliminate the moment. Try to combat sin before it starts.

2. Don't let shame impede your strategic thinking. Attack sin when it's small, so it doesn't it grow.

3. Paddle upstream towards good gifts. Sin can look appetizing, but it can lead to destruction and way from the good gifts God has for you. James 1:17 tells us that every good and perfect gift comes from the father.

Every lie we have believed is the same lie from the garden played repeatedly. When we walk out of slavery and Egypt (metaphorically) and develop a sensitivity to what's going on, we can walk out from underneath the soul ties that are holding us back. Joshua Eze, a holistic success and alignment coach, has a lovely seven-day devotional around soul ties and how to become soul free.

1. Day 1: Awareness – What has me tied? John 8:36
2. Day 2: Ownership – Where did this begin? Lamentations 3:40
3. Day 3: Forgiveness – Release them and you. Colossians 3:13
4. Day 4: Repentance – Breaking the agreement. Acts 3:19
5. Day 5: Renunciation – Tearing down the tie @ Corinthians 10:4
6. Day 6: Rebuilding- Who am I without that tie? Ephesians 2:10
7. Day 7: Releasing – Walking free Galatians 5:1

Always think of how God shakes us before he opens us up to a new process or season. Part of this comes with releasing all soul ties to walk in continual freedom. The seven-day devotional above shows you how important it is to get rid of anything holding you back. The devil sifts us, but God shakes us. In sifting, the enemy steals from us, but God always restores what the enemy has stolen. In the shaking, God awakens us, breaks off what is not of him, shatters bondages (soul ties), and salvages his greatest treasures.

Recognizing What's at Play

God over time can develop people's sensitivity to what is going on. Whether it's a spirit of fear, rejection, pride, etc., understanding what you are dealing with will help you navigate life more freely. For example, I always pray for understanding about what someone is dealing with when I am praying for them. I will normally ask a person what is going on, how we can pray, and as they explain the situation to me and my prayer partners in healing rooms, it may become apparent it's a spirit of fear causing the OCD or anxiety or it's stress causing the worry and the person to break out in a rash. Most diseases have some form of spiritual root. Getting to the root of any issue will help us know how to walk alongside others and navigate freedom better.

I still remember a friend who passed too soon, at age sixty-three, from cancer. She lived an amazing life telling all her doctors about Jesus as she progressed through her health journey. I also know she had a life of tremendous abuse, and I always wondered, *If she had walked through inner healing and deliverance, would she have faced the cancer? Or could it have been prevented?* I also think of my aunt who was diagnosed with breast cancer at eighty-six years old and ended up with a mastectomy. As the Lord had me pray over her, he told me the cancer was because of bitterness in her life. She has been a very bitter woman with a ton of unforgiveness from the pain caused by her husband, who refused to love her. She desperately wanted to be loved, but to this day she does not quite grasp how much the Lord loves her. I say all of this with tremendous love and respect for both women, and God loves them so much; one has graduated to heaven and is fully healed, and one is still alive because her time isn't done yet.

Go back to how much we allow all these root lies to cause the diseases that rage in our bodies. If we would just ask the Lord up front regarding a sickness or health issue what's really going on, the world would be a different place. More miracles, healings, and revival are coming to the world ahead of the Lord's return, and I can't wait to see this come into fruition in the coming years.

The Truth: Christians Can Demonically Oppressed

What's important for us to note is that every case of demonization involves someone under the influence or control, in varying degrees, of an indwelling evil spirit. The word *demonization* is never used in the New Testament to describe someone who is merely oppressed, harassed, attacked, or tempted by a demon. In every case, reference is made to a demon either entering, dwelling in, or being cast out of the person. Matthew 4:24 and 15:22 at first appear to be exceptions to this rule of nonbelievers being the only ones who can be demonically oppressed, but the parallel passages in Mark 1:32 and 7:24–30 indicate otherwise. Hence, to be "demonized," in the strict sense of that term, is to be inhabited by a demon with varying degrees of influence or control.[12]

In Sam Storms second article on this topic, he states, 'It would seem, then, that the debate reduces to the question of the location of demonic spirits relative to the believer, rather than to their influence. In other words, all must concede that Christians can be attacked, tempted, oppressed, devoured, and led into grievous sin. Satan can fill our hearts to lie, he can exploit our anger, he can deceive our minds with false doctrine. The question, then, is this: Does all this take place from outside our minds, spirits, bodies, or could it arise from a demon who is indwelling us?'

---

[12] Sam Storms, "What Does It Mean to Be Demonized?" March 23, 2023, https://www.samstorms.org/enjoying-god-blog/post/what-does-it-mean-to-be-demonized.

The apostle Paul tells us to stand up against the darkness and to put on our armor in order to be prepared for spiritual warfare. He's very adamant about it in Ephesians 6. However, because of the messiness of deliverance, people have stayed away from setting people free and not living out Matthew16:17.

The question of whether Christians should be involved in deliverance ministry is also a discussion in the church. We believe in active combat, not just passive endurance. James 4:7 says, "Resist the devil, and he will flee from you." This calls for actively opposing and fighting against the works of the devil. The kingdom of God does not advance passively. That said, we are assuming an orderly and biblical approach to deliverance ministry that relies on prayer, fasting, and the work of the Holy Spirit and is devoid of human performance or hype.

Ultimately, this isn't just an academic debate. It has real-world implications. If we deny the possibility of demonization in believers, we risk leaving a significant number of people without the help they desperately need. We want to see people set free, walking in greater holiness, and experiencing the fullness of life that Jesus promised. We believe that the church has been given authority, seated with Christ in heavenly places (Ephesians 2:6), to cast out demons in Jesus's name (Mark 16:17) and to help in this process. This authority is not based on our own power, but on the power of Christ dwelling within us.[13]

Scripture Verses About Demons and Demonization

"When an impure spirit comes out of a person, it goes through arid places seeking rest and does not find it. Then it says, 'I will return to the house I left.' When it arrives, it finds the house unoccupied, swept clean and put in order. Then it goes and takes with it seven other spirits more wicked than itself, and they go in and live there. And the final condition of that person is worse than the first. That is how it will be with this wicked generation" (Matthew 12:43–45).

---

[13] Joshua Lewis, "Can Christians Be Demonized?" Remnant Radio, theremnantradio.com, March 4, 2025, https://www.theremnantradio.com/blogs/can-christians-be-demonized.

"And these signs will accompany those who believe: In my name they will drive out demons; they will speak in new tongues; [18] they will pick up snakes with their hands; and when they drink deadly poison, it will not hurt them at all; they will place their hands on sick people, and they will get well." (Mark 16:17-18)

Spiritual Warfare—Fighting Back

- What's holding you back from understanding the supernatural world and our call to combat evil?

- Do you want to trample on snakes and stand in authority?

- What lie have you internalized and are believing that is causing you not to walk out the truths described in this chapter?

- Deliverance is available to all who call on the name of Jesus. How can you help someone be delivered today?

Prayer

Father, we come against anything unholy in our lives and ask for your power to sweep our house clean. Take out any sin, ungodly thoughts, or unforgiveness that gives rights for the enemy to be in our life. Send your army angels to surround us and our homes as we pray for protection of each area of our lives. We submit them to you. In Jesus's name, amen.

Lie #9: God Doesn't Love Me

"God is putting your name in the ear of someone
who can change your life."
—Real Talk Kim (Kim Jones)

Love is an intense feeling of deep affection, something we can have for people, places, or passions. But Scripture reveals a higher form of love: agape.

Agape love is selfless, sacrificial, and unconditional. It seeks the well-being of others above itself. It reflects the very nature of God—His heart, His character, His unwavering commitment to humanity. Agape is the love God pours out on His children and the love He invites us to extend back to Him and to one another. It is the highest expression of love: a choice, a commitment, and a reflection of God's divine nature.

Biblical love gives us a peace that surpasses all understanding, which comes only from Christ. So when we try to equate human love to biblical love, it doesn't compute. I'm probably the last person on Earth who should write a chapter on love, but I do know about the lie he helped me to untangle about love, which is that he doesn't love me.

With our natural mind, we at times can't comprehend how much he loves us; when we relate our human experiences of love to his love, they don't measure up. The area of love has been a minefield for me for the longest time. It is an area in which I allowed the enemy to take me on a wild ride, including two marriages as well as other relationships which never resulted in the hoped-for outcome. Now I fully realize I'm the common denominator in all this, but God has shown up and showed me how his love—his agape love—changes all things, including my circumstances. No circumstance is too big for Jesus to turn around.

How does the lie "God doesn't love me" come into our lives? Through life situations, experiences, and messages from well-meaning people. People say things or we experience relationships which cause heartache and grief to enter the picture and that is how the lie is formed. Then God shows up and undoes all the hurt and pain when we partner with him.

He wanted to show me how much I meant to him, even if it meant being hidden for a season, only to reveal himself to me later when I came to a fuller understanding of his love. A friend told me once in 2023, "We are loved by God and loved ones until God allows a man worthy to go the distance to get to us. God is prioritizing the protection of your heart because it belongs to him." Place your heart in the hands of God and he will give it to the man who he believes deserves it. Who you are in Christ completes you, and you don't need to receive completion from anybody else.

The Hard Truth of Learning His Love

This is a tiny testimony to what God has done through the healing process in my life. It hasn't been easy; in fact, it's been a very long and arduous road, but in his love and kindness, he brings us closer to the Father heart of God. A friend reminded me of several important realities during this season:

No matter what discernment principle we were learning, you always came forth with great insight. Sometimes hard truths that you were seeing and discovering but always, the process bore fruit *in you.* And then holy cow, the last few years. Some uncomfortable truths and it has cost you and your family far more than you could have imagined stepping into those truths. To trust Him in laying down your marriage, your geographic reality and all daily life as you know it. To disrupt the peace with many who don't understand your journey. What courage you have shown. He does not look at appearances and what man sees, He looks at the heart. And today, He wants you to know, Heather, that true healing, maturity, and growth is a process. For all. Born only of His grace and power. But you have a heart for what is true. You have no shied back from He has laid before you. Your heart has been good soil and if you go to that passage, there is promise for you of multiplied fruit for the one with good soil who is receptive to His seed. To whom has given up, to who has born good fruit will be freely given much more. Seek only what is of Him and you will find Him more than enough. He will be your supply. (emphasis mine).

The Truth: God Does Love Me

As the song goes, "Jesus loves me this I know. For the Bible tells me so. Little ones to him belong. They are weak, but he is strong. Yes, Jesus loves me." God absolutely loves you. It may be hard to wrap your mind around, but it is true. This is where the faith journey starts: understanding that God loves you. God is not an angry taskmaster who shows affection only when you succeed. He is a loving Father who will always love you no matter what. Take time to receive the depth of his love for you each day. Allow his love to heal you, transform you, free you, and lead you to the abundant life he has always longed to give.

We Can't Learn How to Love Until We Learn How We're Loved

Mark 1:9–11 (AMP) tells us, "In those days Jesus came from Nazareth of Galilee and was baptized by John in the Jordan.

Immediately coming up out of the water, he (John) saw the heavens torn open, and the Spirit like a dove descending on Him (Jesus); and a voice came out of heaven saying: 'You are My beloved Son, in You I am well-pleased and delighted!'" The Father loved Jesus for who he was and not what he did. "On whom his favor rests" in Luke 2:14 suggests ongoing favor. Jesus was the beloved of God before he ever did anything on Earth.

God says to us, *"You are my daughter, beloved, and with you I am well pleased."* He said that before you and I were ever formed. The greatest trap in our lives is not success, popularity, or power—it's self-rejection. We think our value is determined by what we do for others. Henry Nouwen said, "Self-rejection is the greatest enemy of the spiritual life because it contradicts the sacred voice that calls us the 'Beloved.' Being the Beloved constitutes the core truth of our existence."[14]

---

[14] Henry Nouwen, "The Trap of Self-Rejection," January 10, 2024, https://henrinouwen.org/meditations/the-trap-of-self-rejection/.

You Are God's Beloved

Will you hear the voice that speaks from the depth of your being in the silence of your heart? *"You are my beloved; with you I am well pleased."* There is a God in whose image you were created. You are infinitely loved. The Lord says to us, "I have loved you with an everlasting love. . . . Neither height nor depth, nor anything else in all creation, will be able to separate us from the love of God that is in Christ Jesus our Lord" (Jeremiah 31:3; Romans 8:38–39). There is nothing you could ever do to make him love you more. Would you claim this as your core truth? Sometimes you carry ungodly values in your core; let God replace those with his truths.

Scripture Verses About God's Love

"So we have come to know and to believe the love that God has for us. God is love, and whoever abides in love abides in God, and God abides in him" (1 John 4:16 ESV).

"We love because he first loved us" (1 John 4:19).

"The LORD appeared to him from far away. I have loved you with an everlasting love; therefore I have continued my faithfulness to you" (Jeremiah 31:3 ESV).

Spiritual Warfare—Fighting Back

Open your heart to the one who knows your name. He loves you beyond measure. Let his grace, mercy, compassion, heart, and goodness permeate you. He wants to love you and bring you into his kingdom. Knowing these truths will set you free.

1. How will you let God love you?

2. What steps can you take toward letting more of God's love into your life?

3. When you are honest about where love has been hard, where was God in those moments? Ask him to show you where he was.

4. Sit and soak in worship music. With your eyes closed, who does God say you are? Let his love permeate your life.

Prayer

Lord, we come before you with an open heart and open hands to receive what you have before us. Our hands are cupped and extended outward, hungry to receive from you. We pray that you would block any provision or resource, any person from depositing what isn't orchestrated by you. For all good provisions and right resources to be aligned by you. We pray against any premature or short-sighted move to fill the desire but that the fullness of your perfect gift would be evident, in your timing and your way. And that each of us would be satisfied – heart and soul satisfied. We pray to be with desire, be with the need and be present with him. We pray to recognize your faithfulness to know what truly satisfies. In Jesus's name and power, may it be as he alone knows is good. Refreshing rains released over each of us and abundant grains shooting upward, evident of his transforming work and Spirit. Beloved, he is well pleased with you. Amen.

Truth: Rattle the Cages

"People only get really interesting when they
start to rattle the bars of their cages.
—Alain de Botton

Shifting the Foundations

Shifting means to move or cause to move from one place to another, especially over a small distance. It also means to change in emphasis, direction, or focus. When God is shifting in your life, he's moving things in small distances to another place. When we let go of all the lies, work to unearth the lies, untangle the lies we believe, and make choices to move toward truth, we enable the Lord to shift the foundation of our life.

When we shake off the fear of man, our own fears, insecurities, doubts, and unbelief, we shift. First John 4:18 says, "There is no fear in love. But perfect love drives out fear" One of the many ways we get rid of the fear of man is to realize who and what is in front of us and ask the Lord to help us discern.

Sometimes it comes in the form of surrounding ourselves with those who believe in the vision for our life. Other times, it's allowing God to shift, or move, people out of our lives and to stop casting our pearls before others who do not deserve to know what is going on in our lives. Some people won't be able to go with us as our lives start to shift. A lot of times, stripping or pruning means there are things we are waiting for on the other side of the pruning. We often get so distracted by fear of man or by what's leaving our lives that we don't allow ourselves to be excited for what's coming. When what's coming on the other side of the shift is important, you will well up with excitement in expectation. Shifting into a new season of life is coming.

Once our foundation in Christ has been solidified and rebuilt structurally, we normally walk out stronger, ready to rattle the cages. What does rattling the cages mean? It means coming into a true understanding of your identity in Christ and walking that out. Do you know your identity, and do you believe what Scripture says about who you are in the kingdom? Do you know you are a carrier of the kingdom? We have been given all authority in Christ: "Then Jesus came to them and said, 'All authority in heaven on earth has been given to me. Therefore go and make disciples of all nations'" (Matthew 28:18–19). The most important principle in having spiritual authority is obedience. Continual obedience to and dependence on God with a fear and awe of God is what rattles the cages.

Rattling the cages of the enemy leads to ground-level warfare. The enemy wants to hide behind lies, but our charge is to set the captives free, including ourselves. This is ground-level warfare. Hebrews 2:14–15 (NASB) says, "Therefore, since the children share in flesh and blood, He Himself likewise also partook of the same, so that through death He might destroy the one who has the power of death, that is, the devil, and free those who through fear of death were subject to slavery all their lives." Here, Jesus showed we are able, in our humanity, to break the power of the enemy and set the captives free. In Matthew 10:8, God's charge is to heal the sick, raise the dead, cleanse those with leprosy.

Living out this verse is how you defeat principalities around you, and it shifts the atmosphere from fear to faith. Ask God, *How do I live this out?* We can't quit and give up. Adjust your expectations and see the results of our prayers—the prayer of faith starts with your words. Prayers of authority come out of your walk. Tiny answers to prayer have to be led by the Spirit. The Holy Spirit wants to get to the root issues and symptoms of your suffering, and until you deal with those, you will stay sick. Luke 10:19 reminds us we can overcome the power of the enemy.

Let's use sickness as an example. God wants us well and wants us healed. Physical sickness can be tied to generational issues, addictions, and curses. Or you may have knee issues because you need to lose a few pounds, you're lacking certain vitamins, or you have a spirit of infirmity. You can ask God, *How else can I pray? What else may be happening?* For the issues of life such as sickness and suffering, that's when your confidence is established and you can adjust your prayers to be on target with him.

"Are You a Kingdom Carrier?"

The enemy wants to hide behind lies. Wanda Alger, one of the pastors of Crossroads Community Church says, "Faith has to do with the whole of your life. Do you really believe the Lord is Lord of every area of your life? He wants you to be free in every area of life. Ask Holy Spirit to do fresh work and to be well. 1 Thessalonians 5:23 "May God himself, the God of peace, sanctify you through and through. May your whole spirit, soul and body be kept blameless at the coming of our Lord Jesus Christ."

To Heal the Body: We need to command sickness to leave. Be well and follow Jesus's example. Holy Spirit comes into our Spirit. "The Spirit himself testifies with our spirit that we are God's children." Holy Spirit instructs our mind, our will and our emotions. We must live from our spirit; we need to establish our identity in Christ. You need to get to know your Healer more than your healing.

To Heal the Spirit: Establish Your Identity in Christ. Proverbs 20:27-28 "The human spirit is the lamp of the Lord that sheds light on one's inmost being. 28 Love and faithfulness keep a king safe; through love his throne is made secure." Do you live with the finished work of Christ already there? Get the word of God in us to live that from the inside out.

To Heal the Soul: Renew your mind and heal our emotions. It's what you believe that will determine how you feel. Emotions are symptoms of good and bad. We have to renew our mind on the truth of who He is and what He has done at the cross. Hebrews 4:12 "For the word of God is alive and active. Sharper than any double-edged sword, it penetrates even dividing soul and spirit, joints and marrow; it judges the thoughts and attitudes of the heart."

Word of God is living and active! Identify what is a lie versus what is God's truth. What is my soul feeling and why? Demonic oppression is where evil attaches themselves. They can hover over us to keep us oppressed or sit on our shoulders and whisper in our ears to discourage and harass us. But God has given you authority over them.

The Stronghold: A belief that is counter to truth concerning your identify and security in Christ. 2 Corinthians 10:4-6. An example of a stronghold is I don't really know if God wants me healed. That will keep you bound to sickness. Fear is one of the first spirits to visit and make you believe that God is not enough. Or you've done it for so long it has become an addiction. Are there some evil spirits that have come in and created a mess? It's disobedience to the Lord. Ephesians 4:26 – don't let anger go down on your sin. Are you going to be tempted to give in and sin? James 1:14-15. Desire gives birth to sin and leads to death. An evil spirit whispers deception, no one is really going to know. That is how sin is fully grown which brings forth death. This is what the enemy is after– he wants to kill your spirit; your hope and he wants to take victory away from you. And so just like an addiction – your own will isn't enough. James 5:15-16.

Humility is saying I need help and to confess it to get free. There is nothing like being free in Christ. This comes from repenting and forgiving your flesh, and soul. Ask the Lord to sanctify your desires to help you rule over your flesh. You can renounce your agreement with the lie and not partner with it allowing it into your life.

Demonic Stronghold: These are formed through repeated disobedience which opens doors to evil spirits. See Ephesians 4:26–27 and James 1:14–15.

- Repent for your actions and renounce your agreement with the lie.

- Humble yourself. Demons are rooted in pride and rebellion against authority. The enemy is an imitator of God's kingdom. Pride is the opposite of humility. So, humble yourself, learn to die to yourself and die to your reputation. There is so much humility in saying I am human and I need help. Please help me Lord

- Pray, *Lord, what lie am I believing? Why am I really believing this? Show me what the lie is.* Ask the Holy Spirit to show you what's going on; this can lead to new paths to get you free and out of a rut.

- Command any demonic influences to leave, replace the lies with truth and walk in freedom.

- Make your pursuit after Jesus. Renew your mind to displace the lies. Ask Jesus to show you the purity of who he is and how he is for you.

- Spiritual authority—invite feedback, no shame or condemnation, we all come back to the cross the same and he will set us free. Honor spiritual authority in your life.

- Feed your spirit with the Word. Keep your house filled with the Holy Spirit; you may not be ready for deliverance.

Now What? Look Ahead with Expectation

You've walked through the shifting season, you've come into a deeper understanding of your identity, and now you practice what you've learned.

The key to keeping your spiritual doors open after shifting during these next forty days, or however many days you feel led to practice, is to practice gratitude and thanksgiving. The Lord says, *"Stop talking about your troubles all the time. Instead, talk about ne and how I am faithful. Talk about how I am fixing all your troubles and working them out for your good."* Use the phrase "but God" whenever the enemy tempts you to feel sorry for yourself. *"Thank me and bless me so that I can roll the snowball of rewards into your life that I have for you. Seek me and ask me what to do to receive the specific rewards I have for you, and I will reveal my strategies that you will need to carry out to reap the fullness of your harvest. Let's go rattle some cages!*

"Now is the time to double down on prayer, for the prayers you pray now are still eligible for my rewards in this season. It is not only the prayers you prayed in the past that will bring you reward, but also the prayers you pray now. You are in my 'receiving line,' and all requests you can get in the sweat and tears you have sown are coming back to you as harvest in this time. Leave your troubles at My feet and do not pick them up again. Pray, fast, and seek me as you believe me for my rewards, and you shall receive!"

The Truth: You Are a Child of the Most High God

Pastor Sammy Rodriguez came to Victory Church in 2023 and had the following to say in his sermon. It was too good not to share because it highlights the truth of why you and I are in Christ.

He's not interested in renovating your past but committed to releasing your future!

A broken praise is still a praise!

A wounded worship is still a worshipper!

A prodigal son is still a son!

A prodigal daughter is still a daughter!

The purpose of God is greater than the brokenness of man!

If it's broken, God can fix it.

If it's empty, God can fill it.

If it's failed, God can restore it.

If it's sin, God can forgive it.

If it's wrong, God can make it right.

If it's crooked, God can make it straight.

If it fell, God can pick it up.

If it's paralyzed, God can make it move.

If it died, God can resurrect it.

Jesus is filling in the cracks in the foundation, healing all the lies. As a child of the most high God, we are called to step into greater things because he brings us up higher to be seated in heavenly places (Ephesians 2:6). He wants us to get our view off the ground and to look up with wonder at what is before us. We are also called to be a royal priesthood, holy and set apart. I love the 7H's Sammy Rodriguez spoke about at our church. They are so true because they spell out our inheritance in Christ. They are Holy, Healed, Happy, Healthy, Humble, Hungry and Honor. (see list in appendix) When you follow these principles and Scripture, it will shift your foundation and enable you to be able to build on solid ground.

The time you spend in God's presence will determine your capacity to manage God's promises! He is our rear guard! Nothing will catch us off guard. He promises not to leave us alone or forsake us. His calling on our lives is to come up higher, to see that his promises are yes and amen. In this next season, have the faith of a child to see his promises come to pass in your life. When you break the cycles, come out from under the lies and walk into his abundant freedom; he will take you further than you can ever dream or imagine. He is just that good. Come see, taste, and believe.

Spiritual Warfare—Fighting Back

1. How is God shifting your foundations? Will you allow

    him to make a way in your life?

2. Where are you holding back from the Lord?

3. Do you believe his promises are yes and amen for you

    and your family?

We pray for everyone who takes a chance to read this book,

that the Holy Spirit will hold you and your family up. Go live for

Jesus and the rest will fall into place. May the Lord wash you with

his precious blood in Jesus mighty name. Amen.

Scripture Verses About Shifting Your Foundations

"Therefore, I tell you, whatever you ask for in prayer, believe that

you have received it, and it will be yours" (Mark 11:24).

"So we fix our eyes not on what is seen, but on what is unseen,

since what is seen is temporary, but what is unseen is eternal" (2

Corinthians 4:18).

"I wait for the LORD, my soul waits, and in his word I hope" (Psalm 130:5 ESV).

The Bible contains numerous instances of spiritual shifts. These moments showcase pivotal transformations in faith and character:

- Jacob's ladder (Genesis 28:10–17): Jacob dreams of a ladder reaching to heaven. This dream signals a pivotal shift in his understanding of God's presence, marking the beginning of a deeper relationship with God.

- Isaiah's vision (Isaiah 6:1–8): Isaiah witnesses God's holiness and majesty in a vision. His resulting awareness of sin and acceptance of God's call signifies a crucial shift in his mission and service to God.

- Moses (Exodus 3): When Moses encounters God in the burning bush, he undergoes a profound shift, transitioning from shepherd to leader of the Israelites.

- Paul (Acts 9): Prior to his conversion, Paul actively persecuted Christians. His encounter with Christ on the road to Damascus transforms him into one of the faith's most influential advocates.

- Peter (John 21): Peter's denial of Jesus, followed by his restoration, signifies a shift from fear to boldness in sharing the gospel.

- The woman at the well (John 4:1–42): A Samaritan woman meets Jesus, leading to her transformation and evangelism within her community. Her shift highlights the power of personal encounters with Christ to change lives. She was the first evangelist.

Prayer

Good morning, Father (Papa), Jesus, and Holy Spirit. We ask for a word from you in this season. We ask for dreams and to dream with you again. Father, continue to show and cultivate our assignments. Reveal any lie in our midst and heal us from the inside out. Help us to chase after you, who have big dreams for us, and what your

heart desires for us. What is on your heart today?

You have kindly brought up Colossians 2:6–7: "So then, just as

you received Christ Jesus as Lord, continue to live in him, rooted

and built up in him, strengthened in the faith you were taught and

overflowing with thankfulness." With overflowing thankfulness, we

pray for you to reveal strategies. You are our river of life. We are

asking you to help us with all we need. It is through you and you

alone that we walk in freedom, forgiveness, and thankfulness. For

all you are doing on the earth, please eradicate the lies, set us on

fire, and bring your kingdom to Earth. In Jesus's amazing and

mighty name, amen.

Soul Tie Appendix

"Writing your ending is not your job—it's God's
job. His story always ends with life, and healing and
tears being wiped from every eye.
—*Women's Pastor at Common Ground Church*

When you believe the enemy's lies, you live a life of "less than." You can live from a place of victory! Just not everyone wants to. This is where soul ties come into play in a believer's life. Soul ties are created in a multitude of ways. When we create unholy ties, it creates issues in our lives that aren't meant to be a part of our stories. These ties can be in friendships, marriages, dating relationships, parent-child relationships, boss-employee dynamics, and list goes on. Where the Spirit of the Lord is, there is freedom. The Lord gave us Isaiah 61 for a reason—to let us know he sets the captives free. This is when we come to the Father to find freedom. We ask the Lord to protect us from anything hindering us and declare freedom over our lives.

Here are some examples of how soul ties physically affect a person. Fear is based in the stomach and through removing the fear of rejection and man, you can break free from fear altogether. This means setting boundaries in place to no longer be drawn to the wrong relationships and direction. God can also remove mind-bending spirits that can cause people to seek out wrong relationships. We must tell them to leave and be clear when commanding them to leave, asking God to restore our soul in the name of Jesus. Demons and evil spirits can come int out lives via another person and be shared through experiences or ungodly bonding. We tell the shared demons to be gone in Jesus's name. Our goal and hope is to set the emotions in order: body, soul, spirit, mind, and will. We are to repent on our end to any part where we opened a door, fulfilling a need that only God can fulfill. There can also be progression toward a negative soul tie. Sometimes we feel like we need those people in our lives, and that is not always true. We have to put those thoughts to death.

Secure attachment is positive and healthy. When you have sex outside of marriage, it has an emotional and spiritual impact. Jesus's blood can break it—every inch by the Holy Spirit, his real authority. God will give you more than Satan can take.

1 Samuel 18:1 says, "After David had finished talking with Saul, Jonathan became one in spirit with David, and he loved him as himself." First and foremost, the Lord wants us to be knit together with his heart, and that's where all healthy attachment starts. Our affection should be tied to him first (Matthew 22:37). God does have an order. After God there can be a marriage relationship, then the children, then friends, workplace, etc. When we operate in honor, it's healthy. We usually operate in an unhealthy mode because of unmet emotional needs. How powerful our emotional longings are.

Unhealthy Soul Ties: Relationships That Go Outside God's Order, Honor, and Design

Adult to parent—some needs as a child are never met. Adults sometimes are still longing for affirmation from their parents. The enemy's goal is to take our eyes off the Lord so we are not cleaving to him. Codependency is where we believe the lie, "I can't do without this; I'm not getting it anywhere else, and God's not giving it to me, but this person is." This opens the door for the enemy to come in and just start twisting our belief system.

This excessive reliance can thrive in many areas of our family dynamics, our friendships, our marriages and even with our co-workers. It's one of many devices the enemy uses to steal, kill and destroy the lives of Christ followers (John 10:10).

Are you stuck in a destructive relationship dealing with hurt, fear, lust, and anguish? Many believers do not recognize the source of the destruction. The demonic realm works strategically when it comes to their assignments against us so that they can create open doors for torment. We teach that individuals create these bonds through sexual sin or relationships where someone has ungodly control over us. Sometimes these relationships develop because we allow them to happen and do not set proper boundaries.

Dr. Henry Wright says self-pity is the superglue that binds us to hell. If that is true, then ungodly soul ties are the bungee cords that link us to demonic spirits, attacking us through our friends, families, and coworkers. We may not know it, and we may not see it, but once we understand how this works, we can cut the cord and untether yourself.[15]

One Flesh in and out of Marriage

When you have sex, the creation of one flesh is extremely powerful—not just in the physical but in the spiritual because when you join with one flesh, it means you're joining everything, physically, spiritually and emotionally, and you will receive or inherit whatever that other person is carrying. Now the enemy has access. Cut the tie and renounce the joining together of one flesh (if outside of marriage) and realize that it is another person. In the

---

[15] Jan McKee, "Codependency: A Fruit of Ungodly Soul Ties," Above and Beyond Christian Counseling, accessed December 8, 2025, https://www.aandbcounseling.com/codependency-soul-ties/#more-35527.

power of confession of sin and of forgiveness, he will free us—we don't have to be bound to these things. Acknowledge, "I messed up, but I want to make it right, God, because I want to be free."

No relationship should be above the Lord. I want you to experience the fullness Christ has for you. Confess it, cut it out of your life, and don't look to that other person to meet a need that he or she wants to meet. Cleanse your heart, as Psalm 51:10 suggests.

Steps to Set Your Mind in Advance to Win

1. Ask God to fill you with his love, before you entertain friends or family. The purpose is to walk into God's presence and allow his character to overtake you. Ask God to anoint your head with oil so that no weapon will be able to form against you. Love is the only weapon that will put hot coals on the enemy's head.

2. Bind the demonic spirits operating in the lives of those people you have soul ties with, and loose the fruit of the Holy Spirit before you see them. Speak out loud: "I bind every manifesting spirit from tormenting (name) right now with the blood of Jesus Christ. I loose the fruit of love, joy, and peace into their lives in Jesus's

mighty name." Binding and loosing are our kingdom keys to use. Remember you're not casting the spirits out; you are binding them for a short period of time so they do not taunt you.

3. Break the ungodly soul ties by speaking out loud, "I break the ungodly soul tie between myself and (name). I plead the blood of Jesus Christ between us and cancel every scheme of the enemy in advance."

Remember, as iron sharpens iron, so a man sharpens the countenance of his friend (Proverbs 27:17). God knows your heart, and as you set your path to line up with his plan for your life, he will guide your steps to healing old relationships and establishing new ones.[16]

Godly soul ties are based on love and trust. Ungodly soul ties are based on control and manipulation. You can have both a godly soul tie and an ungodly soul tie within the same relationship. Any control that uses fear, guilt, or shame to manipulate you opens

---

[16] Phyllis Tarbox, "How Ungodly Soul Ties Lead to Ungodly Behavior," Above and Beyond Christian Counseling, accessed December 8, 2025, https://www.aandbcounseling.com/ungodly-soul-ties-lead-ungodly-behavior/#more-30191.

a door that allows demonic spirits to influence your mind, will, and

emotions. That ungodly soul tie becomes a neon sign in the spirit

realm directing more demons your way. You become a banquet

table that was not set by the Lord. Your fear is feeding a spirit of

control and that control is feeding your spirit of fear. Demons come

to grow and gain torment in order to kill, steal, and destroy (John

10:10).

The 7 H's to Remember Your Inheritance in Christ

1. **Holy** 1 Peter 1:7 "These have come so that the proven

   genuineness of your faith—of greater worth than gold,

   which perishes even though refined by fire—may result

   in praise, glory and honor when Jesus Christ is

   revealed."

2. **Healed** 1 Peter 2:24 "'He himself bore our sins' in his

   body on the cross, so that we might die to sins and live

   for righteousness; 'by his wounds you have been

   healed.'"

3. **Happy** John 15

4. **Healthy** 3 John 3 "It gave me great joy when some believers came and testified about your faithfulness to the truth, telling how you continue to walk in it."

5. **Humble** Matthew 5:23–24 "Therefore, if you are offering your gift at the altar and there remember that your brother has something against you, leave your gift there in front of the altar. First go and be reconciled to your brother, then come and offer your gift."

6. **Hungry** – Isaiah 55:1 "Come, all you who are thirsty, come to the waters; and you who have no money, come, buy and eat! Come, buy wine and milk without money and without cost."

7. **Honor** Ephesians 6:1–4 "Children, obey your parents in the Lord, for this is right. 'Honor your father and mother'—which is the first commandment with a promise—'so that it may go well with you and that you may enjoy long life on the earth.' Fathers, do not

exasperate your children; instead, bring them up in the training and instruction of the Lord."

Developing and Living in Emotionally Healthy Spirituality

I.   The Pathway to Emotionally Healthy Spiritualty.

    A. Becoming your authentic self – looking beneath the surface.

    B. Breaking the power of the past

    C. Letting go of power and control

    D. Living in brokenness and vulnerability

    E. Receiving the gift of limitations.

    F. Embrace grieving and loss

    G. Stopping to breath the air of eternity (Sabbath and spiritual rhythms)

    H. Learning new skills to love well – making incarnation your model for loving well.

    I. Loving Jesus above all else.

II.   Practical Resources.

   A. Daily office

   B. Sabbath keeping

   C. Rule of life

www.ingramcontent.com/pod-product-compliance
Lightning Source LLC
Chambersburg PA
CBHW070716130626
46553CB00005B/2013